DR. ALLEN R. HUNT

The

21
UNDENIABLE
Secrets of
MARRIAGE

TAKING *your* **RELATIONSHIP** *to the* **NEXT LEVEL**

DynamicCatholic.com
Be Bold. Be Catholic.®

THE 21 UNDENIABLE
SECRETS OF MARRIAGE

Printed in the United States of America. [1]

ISBN: 978-1-942611-13-4

Dynamic Catholic® and Be Bold. Be Catholic.®
and The Best Version of Yourself® are
registered trademarks of The Dynamic Catholic Institute.

Design by Jenny Miller

For more information on bulk copies of this title or other books
and CDs available through the Dynamic Catholic Book Program,
please visit www.DynamicCatholic.com or call 859-980-7900.

The Dynamic Catholic Institute
5081 Olympic Blvd • Erlanger • Kentucky • 41018
Phone: 1–859–980–7900
Email: info@DynamicCatholic.com

TABLE OF CONTENTS

Daily Secrets

Crucial Secrets

Grace Secrets

GOD'S PURPOSE IS
TO MAKE THE SOUL GREAT.

Saint John of the Cross

WITH THANKS TO...

*Laurie Bolen, Claire Darnell,
Jake Darnell, Andrew Farr, Dee Gipson,
Ryan Lovett, Vinita Wright and many others who
have offered wisdom from their unique
and valuable perspectives.*

BUT MOST OF ALL...

*with thanks to Anita, for she has taught
me more about love and marriage than
I ever could have imagined.*

Note: Individuals and couples cited as examples in this work are all real,
gathered from a variety of sources, including my own life.
However, unless otherwise noted, all of their names and circumstances
have been modified to protect their identities.

THE REASON

I am embarrassed to admit it, but it's true. When my wife, Anita, and I were celebrating twenty-five years of marriage, I finally understood a crucial secret about life. Frankly, it should not have taken twenty-five years for it to become so obvious to me.

What's the secret? *Your decision to marry will almost certainly be the most significant and influential decision of your life.*

There it is, in plain words. A truth almost no one will speak out loud.

Why is your marriage decision so important? First, because your marriage will bind you in a relationship so close and so intimate that it will profoundly shape your whole future. Second, because your marriage will also deeply impact and affect the lives of the people around you for the rest of your life. In fact, this one crucial decision—the selection of your husband or wife—will not only influence every aspect of your life; it will also affect your entire family (your parents, your siblings, your children, all of them) in ways you cannot anticipate, well after you are dead and gone.

Just think for a moment about a few key figures from the Old Testament. Jacob invested more than fourteen years to marry Rachel, and that patience set him up for a fruitful life. Samson, on the other hand, continually fell in love with various women. In the end, that proved to be his demise. King David allowed his eye to wander and became captivated with Bathsheba. His effectiveness as a leader never recovered. Solomon refused to obey God, married non-Hebrew women, and critically damaged his own reign as king.

Again, your decision to marry will almost certainly be the most significant and influential decision of your life. Perhaps that's why Proverbs 4:23 reminds us, "With all vigilance guard your heart, for in it are the sources of life."

There's no denying the truth. Marriage has a potent impact on your life. Marriage can help you become the-best-version-of-yourself and get to heaven. Or it can slowly erode you from the inside out, like some kind of relational Chinese water torture. With so much at stake in a single decision, it seems obvious that you would want to gain wisdom on marriage from every helpful source you can.

I've earned a Ph.D. from Yale University, pastored an evangelical megachurch, hosted a nationally syndicated mainstream radio show, and written several Catholic bestselling books after being received into the Church. I've also been married to the same woman for more than twenty-six years. These experiences have given me wonderful opportunities to view, study, and aid marriages from a perspective that is up close and personal.

As a result, this book combines wisdom from many sources. These secrets come from:

- *my twenty years of working with couples as they decided whether to marry, as they worked through the normal challenges of being married, and as some struggled with marriages in crisis;*
- *my coaching of marriages while hosting a national mainstream radio show for eight years;*
- *the saints, sacred Scripture, and Church teaching;*
- *world-renowned marriage researchers;*

- *and from listening to couples while I've been leading Dynamic Catholic's Passion and Purpose for Marriage events to enrich relationships across the country.*

Your life and relationship will be enriched by these undeniable secrets of marriage.

The Church teaches that God Himself is the author of marriage, and that marriage has been "endowed by him with its own proper laws." (*Catechism* 1603) My search for the secrets of marriage comes from a deep desire to understand God's laws for the relationship between a man and a woman.

Now, as my wife and I celebrate twenty-six years together, and with my own daughters moving toward marriage in their own lives, I am writing down these secrets for all to share. These twenty-one secrets of marriage make all the difference.

Embrace them and you will embrace life.

THE INSPIRATION

When I first heard the story of the marriage of Carlton and Maggie many years ago, I said to my wife, "That's what I want." Anita and I found their marriage so compelling that it painted a mental picture we have used ever since as a model for our own marriage. You will discover their intimate story for yourself in the first chapter of this book.

In many ways, what follows is inspired by that lifelong, life-giving love story. Their story moved me. I think it will do the same for you.

The twenty-one secrets shared here can make that same kind of life-giving marriage a reality for each and every one of us. And that is what we all hope for, isn't it? A marriage that makes us better-versions-of-ourselves? A marriage that gives life both now and eternally?

I sat with Max in a coffee shop. He was preparing to get married for the third time. Regret hung heavy as we spoke together. Reflecting on his two failed marriages, Max said, "I'm like a teacup that sat on top of the mantel before it was knocked off. When it fell to the ground, it broke into several pieces. You can put the pieces of that teacup back together and use it again. But you will always see the cracks where it has been glued together. I've been cracked and will always carry that with me."

No one expects a marriage to fail. No one desires to carry the burden of regret for the rest of their lives. Deep down, every couple who gets married hopes for the best. The best version of marriage. The best dreams for their lives together. The best blessings God can bestow on a couple and a family. And the best outcome, like that modeled in the relationship between Carlton and Maggie in chapter 1.

Read this book. Each chapter focuses on a secret. Study these secrets. Talk about them with your spouse. Consider creating a group of like-minded couples to discuss them together. Embrace these secrets in every way you can.

To help your marriage grow to the next level, at the end of each chapter, you will find a recommended simple exercise to do as a couple. Each exercise is designed to give you a first taste of the power of that secret in your own relationship.

To a couple, I recommend that you read this book together. For example, you might read one secret and then do its related exercise each day for twenty-one days in a row. Or you may prefer to read and share one secret per week for twenty-one weeks. Perhaps you will read and share one secret each Sunday as a part of your day of rest and worship. You may also find that sharing these secrets as part of a book or discussion group in your parish or neighborhood will provide the perfect setting and accountability to propel your relationship (and friendships) forward. When you do dive into these secrets, you will discover that your marriage has grown forward in a brand-new way.

And then the best will be yet to come.

I. MYSTERIOUS SECRETS

"You looked with love upon me
and deep within your eyes imprinted grace."

SAINT JOHN OF THE CROSS

01

THE SECRET OF PURPOSE

If you're going to be married,
you have to know where you're going.

Blessed is the couple who understands their marriage as a pathway to heaven.

Carlton and Maggie met almost a hundred years ago in the rolling foothills of southern Ohio, near the Ohio River. Carlton was nine years old when his father gathered the kids in a wagon to go to a funeral. A neighbor had died, leaving behind a widow and four small children.

After the funeral, as children moved around the burial site, Carlton noticed little seven-year-old Maggie standing with her grieving family. "That's sad," he thought, "such a poor thing, now with no daddy." And Carlton right then vowed to himself to keep an eye on her in the days and years ahead.

Soon, Carlton and Maggie saw each other every day. They were both part of a group of kids who walked to school together each day, traveling a mile down the road to their one-room schoolhouse.

Their friendship grew as each year passed. Carlton finished eighth grade and quit school so he could help his family tend the corn on their farm. Maggie eventually became a teacher in the rural schools of Ohio. They began courting. And together they went to church.

When Carlton turned twenty-four, he left the farm and moved to Pittsburgh to work in the mills. He needed to earn money, more than his family's small farm could provide. So he began as a shoveler. He did well enough that four years later he and Maggie were married.

The couple and their families and friends gathered in the local church. An old retired priest, Father Newman, celebrated the Mass. He had to sit through most of the wedding, since he was past the age of eighty by then.

But Father Newman had a ritual. Before the Mass, he leaned over to Carlton and said, "When I pronounce you man and wife, hold Maggie's hand and don't ever turn her loose." Carlton did just as he was told. *To have and to hold from this day forward.*

Afterward, they all celebrated with cake and lemonade, and the newlyweds spent the night in her mother's home. They visited the next day with Carlton's family, and enjoyed fried chicken and more cake. The day after that, the couple headed to

Pittsburgh, so Carlton could return to work and Maggie could begin settling into her new home.

Carlton went back to work at the mill, in a city filled with smoke belching from the factories. Maggie was lonely in her new environment, and she often reminisced about all the folks back home. *For better, for worse.*

But things got better. She and Carlton found their new parish, with couples their age and friendships that provided fellowship, some of which lasted the rest of their lives.

The Great Depression hit. Carlton's mill remained open, but times were tight. He worked hard. Maggie handled the finances, and struggled to save a nickel here and a dime there. *For richer, for poorer.*

It was not long before they were expecting their first child. And Maggie was fine until one day in mid-May when she was about eight months into the pregnancy.

After breakfast that morning, she doubled over in pain. Carlton rushed her to the hospital. An hour passed, then another. He anxiously kept vigil in the waiting room as the doctor tried, desperately and successfully, to save both Maggie and the baby inside her.

The baby was born breech, and the process did much damage to Maggie's small body, but the nurse brought Carlton a baby boy to meet in the waiting room. He and Maggie named the boy Thomas and called him Tommy.

Maggie and Tommy stayed in the hospital for another week. When they came home, little Tommy wouldn't nurse well. Carlton and Maggie tried everything they could think of to get him to eat.

They took Tommy back to the doctor, who said, "This baby's gotta have breast milk, or we'll never raise him." The doctor suggested that Maggie drink Malt-Nutrine, but the cost was simply too high for Carlton and Maggie to afford. So the doctor asked, "Can you make home brew?"

Carlton replied, "No, but I can learn fast."

And learn he did. Carlton soon found that he could produce eighty bottles for a dollar, and Maggie drank three bottles each day. Finally, her milk fully came in, and Tommy began to grow. The crisis of Maggie's birth and Tommy's struggle to thrive only deepened the love that Carlton and Maggie shared.

The years passed quickly, with Carlton putting in long hours at the steel mill and working his way up the ladder from shoveler to supervisor. Tommy grew up. He went to college, joined the army, was stationed in California, and got married.

Eventually, Carlton retired, and he and Maggie soon moved to Fresno, California, to be near Tommy and his family. The pace of life slowed for Carlton and Maggie. They registered in the parish there and watched their two granddaughters grow up.

The calendar moved forward. Carlton cared for Maggie through breast cancer, cataract surgery, and two broken hips. Eventually, he did all the cooking. He washed, dried, and folded the clothes. He bathed her, because her vertebrae had collapsed from osteoporosis. *In sickness and in health.*

One August evening, Carlton turned off the television and they headed for bed, when Maggie collapsed in pain. He frantically called 911 and waited. At the hospital, Maggie had emergency surgery for a perforated ulcer.

Afterward, she simply needed more care than Carlton could give. The family made the decision to move her to Hope Community

Home, a pleasant, caring place not too far from their home. Maggie soon made friends with all the nurses and residents. She was an easy patient, sweet, loving to laugh, and never complaining.

Her room was large enough so that Carlton could bring his rocker from home and place it beside her bed. It was the same rocker they had brought from Pittsburgh. The gentle creak of that chair comforted Maggie as she lay in the bed and Carlton sat nearby.

Maggie grew weaker and weaker. Carlton continued to feed her three times a day. He agonized over whether to move in with her but instead moved in with Tommy and his wife. Three times a day Carlton drove to be with Maggie at the care home. He still fed her each meal. When he gave up his driver's license on his ninety-second birthday, he relied on the city van to drive him to the home so he could feed Maggie each meal and sit in that rocker beside her.

Carlton rinsed her dentures, stuffed pillows around her body in the wheelchair, and gently dried her hair. Each Christmas, he purchased her two new housedresses. He placed flowers in her honor at their church.

Maggie began to get more and more confused. She was not sure who or where she was. The more she failed, the more frantic Carlton became. Finally, after five years of feeding her every meal, he was told by his doctor that he would have to slow down. So he cut back to two visits per day.

On January 23, the family met with the doctor. The news was not good. Maggie had pneumonia, and she had stopped eating. Her body was beginning to shut down. Death was near.

From that moment on, Carlton was at her side constantly, at first saying, "Maggie, don't die. Please don't leave me."

Then, accepting that what she needed most was reassurance, he began saying, "It's all right, honey. I'm right here. This is Carlton. I love you."

January 27 was a Sunday. Tommy went to church and received the Eucharist. Everyone in church knew why Carlton wasn't there. After the Mass, Tommy and their pastor joined Carlton to bring him Communion. They read the twenty-third psalm. Peace settled over them all.

They left. Carlton remained behind.

He leaned against the bed. "Good-bye, Maggie," he said softly.

With her small hand resting in his, just as it had on the day they were married, Maggie breathed her last breath. *Until death do us part.*

A few days later she was laid to rest with a small box at her side. Inside the box was the faded pink dress she had worn sixty-six years earlier on the day they were married, when she had said she loved Carlton enough to share the rest of her life with him.

Although it would have been a privilege, I never got to meet Carlton and Maggie. When their story was shared with me, it was clear they had yearned to help each other get to heaven. They desired to make each other better. Their goal: to await each other on the other side of the river.

They embraced the secret of purpose. They knew the goal, where they were heading. Wisdom teaches, "Begin with the end in mind." In other words, know where you're going. Carlton and Maggie did just that. They knew their purpose (to get to heaven), and they pursued it together in marriage for more than sixty-six years.

Saint John of the Cross wisely shared: God's purpose is to make your soul great. That's purpose.

Most people will live up to, or down to, the expectations we have for them. When two people marry, if they embrace the expectation of making their partner better and helping him or her get to heaven, the marriage will thrive. Even better, if they understand God is at work to make their souls great, they will have a common goal, something to aim at. They know where they are going: to heaven, to God. And that is the highest expectation of all.

Know where you're going. That is the secret of purpose.

REAL-LIFE HELP

> ## Galatians 5:22–23
>
> *The fruit of the Spirit is love, joy, peace, patience, kindness, generosity, faithfulness, gentleness, self-control.*

The *Real-Life Helps* at the end of each chapter in this book are designed to help you embrace the twenty-one secrets in practical ways. Using these suggested exercises on a continuing basis will allow you to remind yourselves of the power of purpose.

Saint Paul's simple sentence in Galatians 5:22–23 captures the traits you will likely desire in your marriage. Love. Joy. Peace. Patience. Kindness. Generosity. Faithfulness. Gentleness. Self-control. These nine words describe the-best-version-of-yourself. They also embody your purpose in marriage: to help your mate grow in these same nine attributes. The Spirit of God desires to lead you and your mate to heaven, and these nine words describe the heavenly you.

Carlton and Maggie lived fully, suffered together, and loved generously and well. Their journey inspired my wife and me. In fact, even though we never met them, we still talk about them often, because they have become our role model for our own marriage. Faithful. Gentle. Kind. Generous. Loving.

Memorize Galatians 5:22–23 today, and say it aloud together as a couple. Then discuss the ways you are helping your spouse experience these nine qualities in your marriage. For example, how are you helping your spouse be more loving? More joyful? More patient? How is your spouse helping you do the same?

Discuss these nine words together. You now have a clear purpose for your marriage. You know where you are going.

For more in-depth help with embracing and implementing these nine attributes, see my book *Nine Words: A Bible Study to Help You Become the Best-Version-of-Yourself.*

"The matrimonial covenant, by which a man and a woman establish between themselves a partnership of the whole of life, is by its nature ordered toward the good of the spouses and the procreation and education of offspring; this covenant between baptized persons has been raised by Christ the Lord to the dignity of a sacrament."

CATECHISM OF THE CATHOLIC CHURCH. 1601, ARTICLE 7

02

THE SECRET OF SACRAMENT

God shows up in the vows. Every day.

Marriage is a mystery. There is something far deeper going on in a marriage than meets the eye.

That's the only word to describe it: *mystery*. What other word could possibly describe what it's like to merge two people into one, to combine two lives into a single whole? Each marriage takes on a life and character all its own, totally unique to that relationship. That is a mystery. And that is the secret of sacrament.

"Mystical union" may be the best possible way to describe a healthy marriage. But "mystical union" is not a phrase we use every day.

However, God desires to have a mystical union with you, a joining of selves, a blending of spirits. Think about it. The Bible is a love story. Really, the Bible from beginning to end is a story of marriage. It begins with the creation story of Adam and Eve, the first husband and wife, in Genesis. The Bible climaxes and ends in Revelation, with the vision of the glorious wedding feast of the Lamb. At that heavenly wedding feast, all God's faithful people will be united with Him once and for all, forever. In a way, the Bible is showing us that God's ultimate desire is to marry us. We are His beloved. We will be His bride. That is a mystical union.

God joins a couple together in marriage just like He will ultimately join you and me to Himself on that final day. Your earthly marriage now is a sacrament because it points toward that final vision of Revelation, when we will be fully married to God. Sacraments, such as baptism, the Eucharist, confirmation, and marriage, all are outward signs of something God is doing inside us. In marriage, He is joining two people together spiritually, just like He will personally do with each of us at the final wedding feast.

> *I also saw the holy city, a new Jerusalem coming down out of heaven from God, prepared as a bride adorned for her husband.*
>
> **(REVELATION 21:2)**

Husband and wife now are like God and His Church will be then. That is a mystery.

That mystery is the secret of sacrament. Two lives really are becoming one. Husband and wife are joining together, not only physically but also emotionally, spiritually, and in every way. Husband and wife will live together, create a life together as a couple, and they will have the potential to partner with God to create new life through children. Husband and wife will rejoice together, suffer together, and age together. Their lives and experiences will become as one, a mystical union. A sacrament. Remember again the words of Saint John of the Cross: God's purpose is to make your soul great. The sacraments are intended to do just that. In other words, the Holy Spirit desires to use your marriage to share invisible grace and inward holiness with your soul. That's what a sacrament does.

Think how often you have heard someone describe divorce as being like a death. That is because a marriage is not like any other human relationship. It is not merely living together; nor is it an agreement or a contract. Marriage offers something far deeper and far more mysterious. That's because of the secret of sacrament.

Richard and Mary married and served in ministry together for decades.. The couple were known for their excellent teaching and leadership. Richard became president of a college and served in that capacity for more than twenty years. He and Mary had friends around the globe and were the envy of many who saw the purpose and passion with which they lived their lives and their faith.

When they were in their fifties, while speaking at an event in Florida, Mary repeated a story just five minutes after she had told it. Richard thought that was odd. It had not happened before. Mary was just fifty-five years old.

Repeating herself in public began to happen every so often, but not often enough to worry much about—until three years later, when Mary went to the hospital for a heart problem she was experiencing. The doctor shared shocking news: She was suffering from Alzheimer's. And thus began the slow erosion of Mary and her remarkable sparkle and gifts.

Still, she accepted public speaking and teaching engagements. She would repeat herself in some settings, forget where she was in others, and mismatch thoughts before crowds, returning home crushed and humiliated by her inability to perform like she always had before. Her Alzheimer's worsened, slowly, like a glacier creeping into the crevices of her brain and her soul.

Soon Richard was scared to leave Mary alone, so they traveled everywhere together. Everywhere they went, if he took his eye off her for a moment, she would wander away. Mary was slipping away, literally and figuratively.

The caregiver at their home quit. The task of caring for Mary simply became too great.

Their travel together soon became just too much for Richard to handle as well. One flight in Atlanta was delayed for two hours. As they waited in the airport, Mary asked the same questions over and over. Every five minutes or so, she would take a fast-paced walk up and down the enormous terminal for no apparent reason. Richard had to jog to keep up with her. After one of those countless walks, a female executive seated across the bench from them whispered to a friend, "Will I ever find a man who will love me like that?"

The stress finally became too much. Richard resigned his post as president of the thriving college. The school's trustees were dismayed at the idea of losing his leadership. They offered to pay for Mary's full-time care so that Richard could continue in his work. Friends told Richard he should simply pay to move her into a nursing home so he could "get on with" his ministry.

Richard steadfastly, quietly refused the trustees' offer. He gently reminded people of the words he had spoken before God forty-two years before: *In sickness and in health, to love and to cherish until we are parted by death.*

So he resigned and took care of Mary, his soul mate, full-time. In his letter of resignation, Richard wrote, "There is duty, there is fairness, there is integrity, but there is more: I love Mary. She is a delight to me . . . I don't have to care for her. I get to! It is a high honor to care for so wonderful a person."

As the years passed, Alzheimer's slowly locked away parts of Mary one piece at a time, thereby shutting down a part of Richard at the same time. Eventually, she no longer knew who he was. But ironically, as her deterioration continued, Richard's love for her deepened, slowly seeping into every opening of his soul.

Yes, he would lose patience. Yes, he would get lonely. Yes, he would find frustration. But something stronger, something deeper, something greater sustained him.

He leaned on his family and friends. He relied on the memories he and Mary had built for years. Most of all, he drank deeply from the love of God.

After a lifetime of loving and serving God, Richard learned to praise Him when days got their darkest and hope faded. Praise brought relief to his heavy, tired soul.

So, even though she was unable to communicate in the final years, when Mary died at the age of eighty-one, after twenty-five years of slowly slipping away, Richard was there, his love for her being nourished by the love God had for them both.

Obviously, a lot of people do not understand the secret of sacrament. One study has shown that when terminal illness strikes, seven out of ten couples will break up. The strain is just too much to bear. Sadly, it is usually the husband who leaves, just at the moment when he is needed most. In many of those instances, the husband abandons his wife because he has a selfish understanding of marriage. Marriage is about him and what he wants rather than the secret of sacrament.

How do you avoid that tragedy? By embracing the secret of sacrament rather than recoiling from it. Richard understood that he was helping Mary get to heaven by loving her and helping her finish her life as well as possible. He also discovered that serving her in her suffering was helping him become a better person too. His soul was slowly becoming greater with each passing day. In serving her, Richard found the opportunity to grow more gentle, more kind, and more generous. That growth helped him experience love in this life and love from God at a level he never would have discovered otherwise.

Was it easy? Of course not. Was it worth it? Absolutely. When love deepens and blooms more fully, it is a beautiful thing to watch.

When a couple really discover that they are living a sacrament, that discovery transforms their relationship. They immediately enter a new level—deeper, richer. The divine is at work in them and through them. They are not only partnering together; they are also partnering with God.

Richard and Mary embraced the secret of sacrament not only on their wedding day, but in each day of their marriage as God showed up in their wedding vows.

When I heard their remarkable story, I realized not everyone lives by the motto "If it feels good, do it." There simply are some things more beautiful than having volumes of knowledge or sophistication. Some things are more important than doing whatever you want and just trying to have fun.

The most beautiful word of all is love. Not just any love, but agape love. Love that sacrifices. Love that gives. Love that puts the other person before self. Just like Jesus loved and still loves us. The love embodied on the cross. That is agape love.

In a world passionately pursuing self-fulfillment, God shows us there is so much more.

But I shall show you a still more excellent way.

If I speak in human and angelic tongues, but do have not love, I am a resounding gong or a clashing cymbal. And if I have the gift of prophecy, and comprehend all mysteries and all knowledge, if I have all faith, so as to move mountains, but do not have love, I am nothing. If I give away everything I own, and if I hand my body over so that I may boast but do not have love, I gain nothing.

Love is patient, love is kind. It is not jealous, love is not pompous, it is not inflated, it is not rude, it does not seek its own interests, it is not quick-tempered, it does not brood over injury, it does not rejoice over wrongdoing but rejoices with the truth. It bears all things, believes all things, hopes all things, endures all things.

Love never fails. . . .

So faith, hope, love abide, these three; but the greatest of these is love.

(1 CORINTHIANS 12:31FF)

Unfailing, generous, sacrificial love. Love that ripens and matures over time. Love that reflects the active love of God in a relationship. That is the secret of sacrament.

REAL·LIFE HELP

When a computer programmer wants to write a new program, he needs to know what he is trying to create. In the same way, in a marriage, it is crucial to know what the two of you are trying to build.

What kind of marriage do you want to be? Take a moment to discuss this together and write down your answer in your own words. Another way of thinking about it is to ask each other to describe what type of relationship you want to build. You might use the stories of Carlton and Maggie and Richard and Mary as examples. Remember also the nine words from chapter 1 and the importance of sacrament from chapter 2. These examples can all aid you as you write down the marriage the two of you desire to build.

When you find the answer to that question, you have established your core priority. Having this core priority will help you make decisions, and the hard decisions in your marriage will become less challenging because you will know what kind of marriage you want to be. When you struggle with a decision as a couple, bring it back to your core priority and ask, "What decision will help us grow toward the marriage we want to be?"

In addition to having this core priority for your marriage, you may find it meaningful to renew your wedding vows every so often. Use the words you spoke to each other as you performed the sacrament of marriage. This may be as simple as finding the vows you shared at your wedding and reading them aloud to one another right now. Or you may occasionally decide to go a step further and actually schedule a time with your pastor to have him assist you in renewing your vows in a more formal way.

Each time you do this, hear those powerful words again. Let them remind you of the secret of sacrament. Your core priority as a couple, and your wedding vows, serve as a home base that you can return to as often as you desire. They will remind you who you are and who you desire to be. Having these in place is a powerful foundation for your marriage.

Remember that a sacrament is an outward sign of something that God is doing inside you, in your spirit. Just as your wedding rings are visible symbols of your commitment and covenant, so too are your vows a living reminder not only of your commitment to each other, but of God's work inside each of you.

I take you to be my husband/wife
To have and to hold from this day forward
for better, for worse,
for richer, for poorer,
in sickness and in health,
until death do us part.

03

THE SECRET OF SYNERGY

In marital math, one is greater than two.

How can one be greater than two? Everyone knows that one plus one equals two. And everyone knows, of course, that two is greater than one.

However, in reality, one really can be greater than two. That's the secret of synergy.

Pat and Helen taught me this "new math." Married for more than fifty years when I first met them, they lived modest lives. Pat had been a construction worker and manager; Helen served as a librarian for many years before retiring. They had three grown children, all boys, who had families of their own.

In their retirement, Pat and Helen did everything together. They walked together. They read together. They volunteered at their church together. They ate nearly every meal together. Most of all, they gardened together.

It is hard to say whether Pat or Helen enjoyed gardening more. Either way, their garden was the envy of the community. Not too large but not too small, it prospered every year under their care. Pat and Helen grew tomatoes and squash, some corn and some beans, and a host of other vegetables that they generously served up on their dinner table for guests as well as themselves.

But best of all, Pat and Helen grew roses. In fact, their roses were their passion. They experimented with different strains, and each year brought out unique colors and styles from that portion of their garden dedicated to rosebushes. Of course, with their generous spirits, they shared their flowers with everyone. Those beauties appeared on neighbors' front porches, at the church, and in gift baskets that Pat and Helen took with them when they visited friends and relatives.

When our own daughters were born, Pat and Helen arrived soon after with a vase full of fresh roses from their garden. Roses represented life, beauty, and goodness to this couple. Together, the two of them carefully cared for and pruned their rosebushes. Together, they smiled when they shared the fruits of their labor with other people.

Years after we had moved away from their community, my wife and I were invited back to visit. Pat had recently died, and we had not seen Helen since his death. We looked forward to greeting her and checking in on how life had been progressing now that she was living alone.

Early in the evening, Anita and I stopped in to the church to take a look around. To our surprise, Helen was already there. She was placing a beautiful arrangement of her finest roses in the church—red, white, pink, and the extraordinarily lovely Double Delight; simply gorgeous.

Needless to say, we were thrilled to see Helen and delighted to see again the fruits of her gardening skills. I hugged her and said, "Your roses are so beautiful. It is so good to see you and your flowers again."

Helen fussed over the flowers a bit, paused, and then said, "Do you think so? I just didn't know if the roses would bloom without Pat."

She found it difficult to imagine gardening without Pat. He was a part of her, and she a part of him. She really could not see where she ended and Pat began, and vice versa. Two lives, so merged that it was almost impossible to conceive of one living without the other. One had indeed become greater than two. And the flowers embodied that. Together, Helen and Pat had cultivated their roses for years, and they had done so beautifully and fruitfully. But now Helen could not envision how their labors could be divided. Their work alongside each other was like the work of one master craftsman or gardener rather than two separate people.

When asked about marriage, Jesus replied, "'But from the beginning of creation, God made them male and female. For this reason a man shall leave his mother and father and be joined to his wife, and the two shall become one flesh. So they are no longer two but one flesh. Therefore what God has joined together, no human being must separate.'" (Mark 10:6ff)

Of course, it is possible to read this passage as related to sex. "The two shall become one flesh" obviously contains a physical component. And that is certainly part of what Jesus is getting at: the union of two bodies into one that occurs in a loving act of marital intimacy.

But the mystery of marriage goes far deeper than just the physical act of sexual intercourse. A healthy marriage at its best, a holy marriage, does more than merge two bodies into one. Two souls, two hearts, two lives slowly become one. The two complete persons are now one.

That is what the Church means when it teaches that "The consent consists in a 'human act by which the partners mutually give themselves to each other': 'I take you to be my wife'—'I take you to be my husband.' This consent that binds the spouses to each other finds its fulfillment in the two 'becoming one flesh.'" (*Catechism* 1627)

Pat and Helen were no longer merely two loving individuals. They had become Pat and Helen, a unified whole—a one.

Coaches inspire their players with words about how the whole of the team is greater than just the adding up of the talents of the individual team members. That's why championship teams rarely consist of the most all-stars. Championship teams merge the talents of the teammates in a mysterious way so that the team is greater than the parts that make it up. Business executives attest to the same thing. The synergy of parts working together is much more effective than a bunch of great people each working on their own.

The same is true for marriage but in a richer, more spiritual, and deeply intimate way. This mystery of new math, where one becomes greater than two, explains why so many widows and widowers struggle to regain their equilibrium in life after the death of their spouses. It is not just that their "other half" is no longer alive. The loss runs much deeper than that. A part of the very self has been lost too. A part of their thinking, a part of their believing, even a part of their gardening has vanished. Their shared memory has been ruptured. One is indeed greater than two, and when a spouse dies, that remaining one is changed in profound ways. A deep part of the self has been lost.

And the same holds true for divorce. A huddled mass of tears and raw emotion, Kevin sat in my office on the day after his divorce. His wife had left for another man, and now Kevin held his divorce decree as the only remnant of his ten-year marriage. The final decree stated: "It is hereby ordered that the marriage contract . . . is hereby set aside from this date and fully dissolved . . . shall be held and considered as separate and distinct persons, altogether unconnected by any nuptial union or civil contract whatsoever."

Kevin showed me the decree and asked, "How in the world can they say we are unconnected by any union? Fully dissolved? She was my wife, for heaven's sake. She's the mother of my kids. Unconnected? She's a part of me. We'll be connected forever." In the years after that, whenever I saw Kevin, he never failed to mention that he had lost a part of himself that he could never get back.

Research shows that as two people merge into one, they live life differently. In particular, their intelligence as a pair expands and becomes far larger than it could ever be as two individuals living on their own. As a married couple, they can take each other to new places. They can expand their imaginations and share life events, like childbirth, travel, and even trauma, that serve to expand intelligence. Once those experiences are shared, and merged with day-to-day living, they become a permanent part of who you are as a person and as a couple.

Our combined intelligence expands in practical ways as well. For example, the husband may begin to count on his wife to handle all things monetary—not only to pay the bills but also to keep abreast of the trends in retirement investments, interest rates, mortgages, and credit cards. She gathers the information for the family regarding finances. A wife may count on the husband to gather wisdom and lead in the area of spirituality. The family may look to him to find helpful ways to incorporate prayer, service, and the faith into their life together.

The merging expands in a new way with the addition of children. One child may be the member of the family relied upon to discover and absorb new developments in technology, like the latest version of the smartphone or apps to help the family find movies or entertainment. "Can you help us understand our phone bill, please?" Another child might be the one who absorbs information regarding navigation: analyzing maps, finding interesting places and parks to visit, and discovering tools that assist in the travel itself. "What kinds of fun stuff might we do for vacation this year?"

What social scientists have found is that couples, and then their families, instinctively divide areas of information and begin to rely on each other. It's as if they outsource different kinds of information to different members of the family. They do this so much that a kind of collective intelligence emerges for the whole unit that no single person could replicate due to limited time or abilities. In fact, when a mother or father dies, or a divorce occurs, the entire family struggles because part of their intelligence and information-processing abilities has disappeared. In a very real way, this collective intelligence demonstrates another way in which one is far greater than two. In a way, the surviving spouse or family becomes less intelligent because they have lost part of their information-gathering and absorbing process. One as a pair is greater than two on their own.

This is certainly true for Anita and me when it comes to relationships with other people. We both are extroverts, but in different ways. I love to meet new people and have short conversations. I'd be the perfect Walmart greeter. In fact, that is my retirement plan! Best of all, I remember names, nearly always. Anita, on the other hand, cannot remember names at all. But she is strikingly accurate at assessing people, their character, their strengths, and their trustworthiness. We both enjoy people, but together we make each other better. I remember the names, and she understands them in a deep way. But also, together we are better than we are alone. One is greater than two.

This mysterious merging occurs in healthy marriages. It is what Jesus meant when He said, "the two shall become one." One really is greater than two. Pat and Helen proved that. So did their roses.

That is the secret of synergy.

REAL·LIFE HELP

As you read and reflect on the passage from Mark 10:6ff ("'God made them male and female. For this reason a man shall leave his mother and father and be joined to his wife, and the two shall become one flesh.'"), read aloud and pray the following prayer together. Find a way to use it each day for a week. You might place the prayer on the mirror as a reminder, or use it together at a meal or before going to bed each evening.

PRAYER OF A MARRIED COUPLE

Thank You, Lord
For the meeting of
Our hearts
Our lives
Our souls
All is yearning
All is hope

Come bless our lives
You who see into future ways
With Your eternal wisdom
Protect our nights and days

Make our home
A place of joy
When storm clouds gather
Let no hurt destroy

May Your Angels
Find a home from Heaven
Therein
When days are sad
May we hear them sing

May friends young and old
Cross this threshold to find
A sacred embrace
A welcome in kind

Lord of Love
May we know
The gift of Your Spirit
In times of strength
In times of sorrow

When hearts are strong
When hearts are hollow
Whisper courage to the wind

May the harvest of our lives
Mellow our hearts
Where silence is sacred
And words can depart
For You are there
Keeping watch
In our twilight years

This is but the beginning
Of love in eternity
Beyond, Above, Below
How could we ever know
The depth of Your love

Till death do us part . . .

What is death
Only finding love
Beyond the stars.

(FR. LIAM LAWTON)

II. REVOLUTIONARY SECRETS

"Patience achieves everything."

SAINT TERESA OF ÁVILA

04

THE SECRET OF BEDROCK

———

For a marriage to work, it is important to share everything, including the deepest values in your heart.

The secret of bedrock may perhaps be the greatest gift I can give you in this book. It's so vital that I nearly placed it first.

Plenty of research shows that this secret will be the strongest predictor of the success of your marriage. Priests and pastors will recommend that any relationship start with it. Without the secret of bedrock, your foundation will be unsteady. It may last, but it will always have wobbles in the structure that will prevent your marriage from standing strong and steady, as you deeply yearn for it to do.

What is the secret of bedrock? Prayer. Prayer that leads to a spiritual life together as a couple. A spiritual life together that will give you the same values and convictions in your heart so that the two of you are driving your relationship in the same direction at the same time in all settings. A deep melding will bind you together as a couple, and that bond will sustain you in ways you can never anticipate at the beginning. Your shared spiritual life will serve as mortar between the bricks of your home, pulling all the various parts together and holding them together as a unified whole.

When your child does not come home one night as expected and you aren't sure how to react, the secret of bedrock will see you through. When you are unable to have children on your own, the secret of bedrock will steady your love for one another and guide you. When your husband gets laid off from his job, or is diagnosed with cancer, the secret of bedrock will be your friend. Most of all, when you face major decisions as a couple, the secret of bedrock will remind you both of what you really value and what ultimately matters, because you believe the same things. You hold the same things dear.

Virtually every study ever done has shown that couples who share the same faith, and practice that faith together, have the lowest rates of divorce. That does not mean that all other marriages will fail, only that they are less likely to stand the test of time and trial. In America, it is increasingly challenging to find a mate who shares your faith and practices it in the same way you do. We have grown increasingly secular and hostile toward religion. We've also grown so multicultural that many people are unwilling to set down deep roots in any one faith and set of beliefs. Instead, they lead their lives as a sampler of many cultures, never sinking deeply into any set of commitments or values.

A University of Texas at San Antonio study found that couples who shared their faith and worshipped together regularly not only reported a higher level of marital satisfaction but also raised that satisfaction level even further when they were active together in other ways at their church. Most of all, when the couples shared prayer and devotional practices at home, their marital satisfaction level ranked the highest of any participants in the study of 1,387 couples.

Add to that a University of Virginia study that found that merely attending worship together as a couple reduces the divorce rate by about 35 percent. Stronger still, a Georgia Family Council survey showed that of couples who prayed together, only 7 percent had seriously ever considered divorce, compared to 65 percent of those who never prayed together. You get the point.

In an era when the length of celebrity marriages is measured in hours and days and the divorce rate is usually quoted as about 50 percent, one thing is clear: Marriage is hard. And when you do not have the same core beliefs, and you do not see your life and the world in the same way, marriage is even harder. In fact, it's almost impossible.

Our own research at the Dynamic Catholic Institute found that when both spouses actively practice their Catholic faith together, the divorce rate is less than 11 percent. In other words, your marriage is almost guaranteed to thrive when you go to Mass, give generously, serve compassionately, and pray together.

When you do those things regularly rather than sporadically, you drop your likelihood of disaster from 50 percent to 11 percent. That's a nearly 80 percent shrinkage in the divorce rate—just from actively practicing your faith together. Shared faith plus shared convictions equals strong marriage. Pretty good results, huh?

For a marriage to work, it is important to share everything, including the deepest values in your heart. Your relationship with God lies at the center of who you are and shapes all you do. When you and your spouse do not share that, you are trying to sing a duet from two different song sheets.

The book of Tobit does not get much airtime in Mass during the year, but in it, you will find a beautiful jewel to remind you of the secret of bedrock. When Tobiah learns that God has chosen Sarah to be his wife, he immediately falls in love with her, without ever having seen her in person. He places his faith in God above all else. His relationship and marriage are placed in the hands of God.

Sarah has been betrothed before. In fact, she's been there *six* times before! And each time, her husband-to-be was slain by a demon on the wedding night. Six times in a row. Not good.

Nevertheless, in spite of this track record, Tobiah trusts in God and His plan. He marries Sarah despite the dangers he's been warned of by every other observer. When the newlyweds face the fear of their wedding night and the proximity of demons, danger, and death, they immediately turn first to the Lord. They get on their knees and pray together.

Tobiah rose from bed and said to his wife, "My sister, come, let us pray and beg our Lord to grant us mercy and protection."

She got up, and they started to pray and beg that they might be protected. He began with these words:

"Blessed are you, O God of our ancestors;
blessed be your name forever and ever!
Let the heavens and all your creation bless you forever.
You made Adam, and you made his wife Eve
to be his helper and support;
and from these two the human race has come.
You said, 'It is not good for the man to be alone;
let us make him a helper like himself.'
Now, not with lust,
but with fidelity I take this kinswoman as my wife.
Send down your mercy on me and on her,
and grant that we may grow old together.
Bless us with children."
They said together, "Amen, amen!"
Then they went to bed for the night.

(TOBIT 8:4-9)

Their relationship is rooted in faith. God lies at the bedrock of the marriage. Tobiah tests his motives for marriage before God: May this relationship be built on faith and fidelity rather than on lust and immaturity. Their marriage not only survives the wedding night, but this beautiful prayer becomes a template for all marriages to follow. Faith and fidelity create marriages built to last.

When you have children, the challenges become even more pronounced. Schedules get tighter, money gets scarcer, kids get older and begin making their own decisions, and the list goes on. The secret of bedrock becomes even more important for your marriage and family. First, you have less attention to pay to one another as a couple. Sharing the same view of God and life will equip you for this season of marriage when you have less time for each other. Second, you will now have little souls who are counting on you to prepare them for life. Only you can grow them into the people God wants and designed them to be. The secret of bedrock will help you build faith into your home life and into your children's souls.

You may choose to build a tradition with your children during Advent to get ready for Christmas. Traditions create meaning and consistency in your family. Long after your children are grown, they will still remember—and often ask to do—the traditions, whether they are lighting an Advent wreath in your home together or serving at the homeless shelter as a family each Thanksgiving.

You could decide to devote a week's vacation each year to serving on a mission team through your parish. You might build a habit of daily prayer and Bible or devotional reading into your home so that your children learn sound spiritual habits. The secret of bedrock can also be expressed like these words from Saint Paul in Colossians 3: "Whatever you do, do it all in the name of the Lord Jesus."

When you build these spiritual habits into your marriage, family, and life, you will create a home that can stand in even the strongest storm. In a way you will become like a man named Tho Bien, who immigrated to America from Vietnam. He married a woman from Germany, and they moved into the California hills and began to build their dream home.

Tho Bien did all the work himself. He poured the foundation. He did the framing. He put the roof in place. He laid the plumbing lines and put in the electrical wiring. Tho Bien did it all. For two years, he labored, buying only the best materials for his work. He wanted his home to be excellent. And he put stucco on the outside to make it fireproof.

When the wildfires came to their area, Tho Bien was ready. Everyone else evacuated their homes. He sent his wife and daughter away, but he stayed with the house he had built. Most of the time, he sat on the roof, pouring water on it to keep it damp and cool. Tho Bien had invested so much of himself in that house that he could not bear to abandon it.

Today, if you go to that area, you will find a hillside ravaged and charred. You will find no trees. Only a few chimneys and toilet bowls remain near the top of the hill. You will also find Tho Bien and his family still living in the dream house he built by hand with only the finest materials. In a way, Tho Bien is like the man Jesus described who built his house upon the rock rather than on the sand. When the storms came, his house stood tall and strong.

When you establish your marriage on the shared values of your faith, and then regularly practice that faith together, you will be stormproofing your life and family. That doesn't mean you will not face challenges; it merely means you will have the strength and depth of resources to weather them.

God is not some vague, distant force to people who pray regularly, but rather a personal friend and adviser. These people are trying to listen to the voice of God in their lives. They know that doing God's will is the only path that leads to lasting happiness in this changing world (and in the world beyond). What is important to recognize is that dynamic Catholics have a time to pray, a place to pray, and a structure to their prayer.

The most straightforward way to do this springs forth from our Dynamic Catholic Prayer Process. When you as a couple develop a prayer habit—it may be as simple as five to ten minutes per day—your marriage will thrive in a way you could never have anticipated. New strengths will emerge, and God will begin to open vistas on your future and your family. Again, the point is to make a simple habit—five to ten minutes a day. An occasional, sporadic prayer here and there ("Oh, Lord, help me find a parking space," or "Oh, Lord, help us get home in this storm") is not a bad thing. But a regular prayer habit is something altogether different. You're pouring the foundation for your life together.

Daily prayer *is* your relationship with God. Without it, there really is no relationship. With no communication, it is difficult to have any relationship, especially a divine one. And when you pray together as a couple, you are inviting God's grace into your life, and His spirit to grow you both forward. Remember, you are helping each other get to heaven.

Here are the basics of the Prayer Process that our team at Dynamic Catholic uses and suggests:

1) GRATITUDE

Begin by thanking God in a personal dialogue for whatever you are most grateful for today.

2) AWARENESS

Revisit the times in the past twenty-four hours when you were and were not the-best-version-of-yourself. Talk to God about these situations and ask him to give you the gift of greater awareness when similar situations arise in the future.

3) SIGNIFICANT MOMENTS

Identify something that you experienced today and explore what God might be trying to say to you through that event.

4) PEACE

Ask God to forgive you for any wrong you have committed (against yourself, another person, or Him) and to fill you with a deep and abiding peace.

5) FREEDOM

Talk to God about how He is inviting you to change your life so that you can experience the freedom that comes from knowing that who you are, where you are, and what you are doing makes sense. Is He inviting you to rethink the way you do things? Is God asking you to let go of something or someone? Is He asking you to hold on to something or someone?

6) PRAY FOR OTHERS

Pray for those you feel called to pray for today, and those who have asked you to pray for them recently. Take a moment and pray for these people by name, asking God to bless and guide them.

FINISH BY PRAYING *THE OUR FATHER.*

Slowly build this simple little habit into your daily life as a couple, and open yourself to a wellspring of God's presence. Then watch as that presence guides you through the roller coaster of experiences that every marriage brings. Best of all, watch that wellspring of your prayer life bear fruit in the lives of your family and children. You will build your house upon the rock.

That is the secret of bedrock.

REAL·LIFE HELP

Just for today, as a couple, use the Dynamic Catholic Prayer Process I've just outlined. Try it one time today for five to ten minutes. Perhaps the wife will pray aloud. Perhaps the husband will lead the time. Do what is most comfortable for you as a couple. No one is keeping score. This is your time with God.

One simple way to begin is to start with Gratitude only on the first day. Then, on the second day, add Awareness. Then add one component of the Prayer Process each day until all the parts are in place.

After today, discuss how you can do this exercise as a couple each day. First thing in the morning usually works best, but that may not work for you for reasons of your own. Find a time and place where the two of you can commune with God. Build a prayer habit. It will be the greatest gift you ever give yourselves and your marriage.

For more details on this Prayer Process, I recommend Matthew Kelly's book *The Four Signs of a Dynamic Catholic*.

05

THE SECRET OF LITTLE THINGS

Marriage is a garden, not a fruit stand. You have to tend it.

Imagine a husband and wife sitting on the couch at the end of a workday. He is completely immersed in *Monday Night Football* and whether the Packers will defeat the Broncos. She sits at the other end of the couch, wrapped physically in a blanket and wrapped mentally in a romance novel. Finally, she breaks the cold silence and says to her husband, "Honey, you never tell me that you love me anymore." The husband briefly looks at her so as not to miss the next play in the game and says, "Sweetheart,

I told you that I love you when we got married. If anything changes, I'll let you know."

If I asked you whether you thought that particular marriage would last, you'd probably chuckle and say no. What is this couple lacking? It's the secret of little things.

Marriage researchers Dr. John Gottman and his wife, Julie, claim to be able to predict with 94 percent accuracy whether a couple will eventually divorce after observing that couple interact with each other for just ten minutes. Ten minutes.

How can they make this bold claim? They look for a 5:1 ratio of positive to negative interactions. A 5:1 ratio as the couple relates to one another. Positive interactions include simple things such as a smile, a touch on the arm, looking directly into your partner's eyes, paying attention to what he or she says, saying thank you, sharing a quick hug or a giggle. Negative interactions include rolling the eyes, turning a cold shoulder, a dismissive harrumph, a mocking chuckle, or failing to listen to or acknowledge what your spouse is saying.

When you read that list, I hope you notice that these little interactions occur all the time throughout the day, in small ways that often become habits. And habits can be easy to form and difficult to break. For example, if I get in the habit of rolling my eyes every time my wife mentions the need for help with some housework, or if I habitually fail to listen to her because I love watching football, changing those habits is going to require some work on my part (not to mention some patience on my wife's part!).

But that is John and Julie Gottman's point. Marriage consists of the little things. Marriages live and die on an everyday basis, but it's not because of one big decision or some grand gesture. Marriage means choosing to love, and loving means action in the little things—not just saying "I love you" at the wedding ceremony and then going back to our regular self-absorbed lives.

When you consider the Gottmans' research, it is remarkable how much their analysis of the little things matches what we Christians should already know. Remember the words of Saint Paul in Colossians 3:12–17:

> *Put on then, as God's chosen ones, holy and beloved, heartfelt compassion, kindness, humility, gentleness, and patience, bearing with one another and forgiving one another, if one has a grievance against another; as the Lord has forgiven you, so must you also do. And over all these put on love, that is, the bond of perfection.*
>
> *And let the peace of Christ control your hearts, the peace into which you were also called in one body.*
>
> *And be thankful. Let the word of Christ dwell in you richly, as in all wisdom you teach and admonish one another. . . .*
>
> *And whatever you do, in word or in deed, do everything in the name of the Lord Jesus, giving thanks to God the Father through him.*

In these words, Paul describes the little things as putting on a different set of clothing. "Put on . . . compassion, kindness, humility, gentleness, and patience . . . forgiving one another . . . love . . . peace . . . and be thankful." Being married is in many ways like trading in your old clothes and putting on a new set.

In fact, that was how early Christians thought about baptism: a changing from the old self to the new self symbolized by a change of clothes.

Your old clothes were mostly about you. When you were single, you could focus most of your energy and attention on yourself and your wants. But now you are married. Your new clothes are all about your spouse and your relationship: the clothing of compassion, kindness, humility, gentleness, patience, forgiveness, love, peace, and thankfulness.

Remember, you build your marriage on positive interactions, and those positive interactions need to outnumber negative ones five to one. For every negative interaction a husband and wife may have, it must be balanced by five positive interactions. In other words, for every unkind word, there will need to be five smiles, thank yous, love pats, attentive listenings, or deep looks in the eyes.

Small things matter because life consists of small things. Most days look an awful lot like all the other days: get up, shower, get dressed, attend to the kids, eat, go to work, run some errands, exercise, commute, etc. And if you are not careful, little habits form, and relationships erode because you establish a pattern of doing things the same way every day. Noticing and being attentive to your spouse may not fit into that schedule. Small things will make the difference. While a really large romantic vacation trip every other year may be a good thing, it will never be able to compensate for two years' worth of negative interactions, cold shoulders, eye rolls, and failing to pay attention to your spouse. Life and marriage consist of the little things.

Saint Thérèse of Lisieux has taught us that the same principle applies to our spiritual lives. Our souls become greater or lesser based on the little things we choose each day. She reminds us, "The only way I can prove my love is by scattering flowers, and these flowers are every little sacrifice, every place and word, and the doing of the least actions for love." In other words, in your faith life, when you make little sacrifices to and for God each day, your soul grows stronger, and your love grows deeper. In the same way, in your marriage, when you choose to make little sacrifices for the benefit of your spouse, your love will deepen and your relationship will grow stronger.

These same little things will accomplish the miraculous. As you act daily like you are fond of and admire your spouse, you actually will become fond of and admire your spouse. As you smile, listen, touch, and appreciate him or her in the small things, your love will deepen and last.

You will also notice that focusing on the little things means you do not dwell on and obsess over your spouse's flaws. The little things will help keep you positive as you appreciate the strengths and good qualities that attracted you to your spouse in the first place.

The little things will also prevent contempt, criticism, defensiveness, and stonewalling from creeping into your marriage and destroying it. The Gottmans call these four issues the four horsemen of the apocalypse. That's because marriages full of contempt, criticism, defensiveness, and stonewalling are in real danger of ending very soon.

When a couple's interactions embody contempt and criticism, things are clearly breaking down. When anger becomes normal and daily, the relationship has broken down. Your very behavior is destroying the person God has entrusted to you. That is not God's will, and it is not OK for your relationship to be dominated by anger and its first cousin, resentment.

Of course, the healthiest marriages have conflict. The question is not whether there will be conflict; rather, the question is how to fight lovingly and well. Thriving marriages share a conflict resolution style that allows the marriage to navigate through the conflicts that come to all relationships. Both spouses may argue loudly and passionately, but then they move on quickly from the conflict, leaving the argument behind as soon as it ends. Or they may be more passive, avoiding conflict or quickly dismissing it rather than dealing with it. But since both spouses deal with conflict in the same way, they move past it together.

Most unhealthy marriages, however, have conflict that never seems to end. Anger and criticism fly around the room in every conversation. The same old hurts keep resurfacing each time. Additionally, some of the unhealthiest marriages have no conflict at all. There is not enough communication for conflict even to occur. As a result, hurts becomes grudges, and grudges fester and grow into resentment. Resentment then leads to contempt and criticism, which act like battery acid, corroding the relationship over time. Rather than deal with conflict, spouses pepper the family conversation with nagging and snide remarks on every occasion.

To prevent that, invest in the 5:1 ratio of positive interactions to negative. Interact early, interact often, interact regularly. Interact in the small, simple things. When you do so, you will discover that a lot of arguments simply will never occur. Criticism will decrease, and affection will increase.

One way that Anita and I try to accomplish this is by walking together. We walk together for thirty to forty-five minutes about four nights a week. Obviously, the exercise is good for our bodies, but the walks are better for our relationship. First, the walks help simply because we are together. Second, our relationship deepens because we use the time to talk about anything and everything, the small, simple things. And we are interacting, listening, looking each other in the eye, smiling, touching, and saying kind things to one another. The walks create a lot of positive interactions for us.

In the same way, we work to have lunch together once or twice a week, based on schedules and travel. The little things may be small, but they matter. Choosing to create positive little things will carry the day in your marriage. Choosing is just that: choosing. Schedule time, like walks or dates, when you will build your habit of little things, and that habit will spill over into your other interactions as a couple.

It is plain from both Church teaching and solid research that love is more about *doing* than it is about *feeling*. It is a choice and a behavior much more than a feeling. When you do love, that is when you will *feel* love.

And as you try to create these five positive interactions for every negative, you will find your marriage growing stronger and healthier. You will be building a marriage that will last. It sounds like a cliché, and maybe it is, but it is true for marriage nevertheless. How you treat each other makes all the difference in the world.

Little positive interactions will help you avoid what I call the Katharine Hepburn mistake. She said, "If a lady wants to give up the admiration of many men for the criticism of one, go ahead and get married."

What's the cure for the Hepburn mistake? The secret of little things.

REAL-LIFE HELP

Invest fifteen minutes in this exercise with your spouse. Sit privately by yourself for five minutes and write down as many of the interactions between you and your spouse from today (or yesterday if you are doing this first thing in the morning) as you can remember. Call to mind each time your spouse interacted with you. What do you recall from his or her treatment of you?

In particular, make note of eye contact, paying attention, touching your hand or arm, smiling, saying thank you or "I love you," and other little ways that your partner interacted with you. Also call to mind times when he or she rolled eyes, ignored you, made fun of you, or criticized you.

Now join with your spouse. Begin with a short prayer and ask God for grace to abound in your marriage. Say something like, "God of grace, help us to be the greatest marriage we can be. Help us to love each other well, and to bring out the best in one another. Amen."

Take a moment now to share your written reflections of your interactions from this day. Do not interrupt each other. Let the wife go first, and share; then the husband. Listen attentively. Then ask each other how you can grow to have more positive interactions. Do not have a lengthy conversation right now. And do not bring up interactions from other days. Just listen and learn from the brief recollections of this one day. Agree to love each other. And close with a second simple prayer. Something like, "God of love and God of forgiveness, thank you for the gift of our marriage. Teach us to love like you love. Amen."

III. DAILY SECRETS

06

THE SECRET OF THE LOVE BANK

————

*If you want more love, you have
to give it away.*

Every person has a love bank inside the heart, one that can either be filled with love or be left bankrupt and empty. And we all yearn for our love banks to be filled to capacity. This is the secret of the love bank.

You can also call the love bank the law of the harvest. As Saint Paul writes, "Make no mistake: . . . a person will reap only what he sows. . . . Let us not grow tired of doing good,

for in due time we shall reap our harvest, if we do not give up."
(Galatians 6:7, 9) Very simply, you will reap what you sow.

For marriages, and even for your life, the application of this
rule is simple: If you want more of something, give it away. If you
want more love in your life, give more love away. If you want more
joy, give away more joy. And it is especially true in marriages.

Marriage researchers such as Gary Chapman and Willard
Harley have written extensively and well about the secret of the
love bank. Here's the truth: God made each of us to love and
to be loved. First, to love Him and to be loved by Him. Second,
to love other people and to be loved by them. In fact, we often
experience God's love most as it comes to us through the people
around us. And if your marriage is a sacrament and expresses
the love God has for you, it only makes sense that you would
experience God's love through your spouse. And that he or she
would in turn experience it through you. Again, God is at work
in the sacrament to make your souls great.

But that's where it can get hard, isn't it? Positive interactions
make deposits into your love bank. Negative interactions
make withdrawals. The five positive interactions for every one
negative (remember the 5:1 ratio from the previous chapter)
help keep your love bank full. And your interactions with your
spouse keep his or hers filled as well, assuming that you know
what love feels and sounds like to your partner.

And that is where we all need some help. Chapman has
described five love languages. Those languages are how we each
give and receive love. And of those five, each of us has two
primary love languages we understand best. But there's the

catch: In all likelihood, your two primary love languages are different from those of your mate.

See this in plain print right now: You and your spouse are different. Shocking, isn't it? Therefore, you probably are not exactly the same when it comes to how you best give and receive love. You and your spouse love differently. Discovering this basic fact fundamentally changed my marriage, because it changed me.

Chapman describes the five love languages as:

1) QUALITY TIME: *Giving and receiving undivided attention*

2) RECEIVING AND GIVING GIFTS

3) ACTS OF SERVICE: *Doing things you know your spouse would like you to do*

4) PHYSICAL TOUCH

5) WORDS OF AFFIRMATION: *Complimenting and encouraging your spouse as a person, both for who she is and for what she does*

Again, it is rare for spouses to have the same two primary love languages. My wife, Anita, gives and receives love best in terms of Quality Time and Acts of Service. She feels loved when I give her my undivided attention, when I listen intently to her, and when I share all the details of my day. That is quality time. And she really feels loved (and gives love) through Acts of Service, when I vacuum, go to the grocery store, or do some chores and errands for her. She especially feels loved when I combine her two love languages and simply accompany her on errands while she is receiving my undivided attention at the same time!

On the other hand, I am like a lot of men. I feel loved when Anita compliments me or shares her admiration through compliments or kind words about who I am. Those are Words of Affirmation. And I feel loved when we share Physical Touch, when she touches me in public, sits near me on the couch and touches me, or when we are sexually intimate. These two love languages are often, but not always, the primary ones for men.

By now, you see the simple complication. How Anita gives and receives love does not match how I give and receive love. It's almost like we speak different languages, as if I were loving her in Portuguese and she were loving me in Polish. We each mean what we say, but the other does not understand the language being spoken. And yet here we are, married and designed by God to love one another. Our vows reflect her love languages: "for better, for worse, for richer, for poorer." And the vows reflect mine too: "to have and to hold."

So, if my love languages do not match hers, what happens? Two things.

First, I will probably start off in the marriage by showing my love for her in my own languages. And that is what I did (and often still do). I complimented Anita, told her how beautiful she was, shared with her how marvelous I found her personality and steadfastness to be, and showed her physical touch. In my mind, I was loving her. To her, those were nice things but not necessarily the most loving.

In the same way, she loved me in her languages, performing acts of service like doing the laundry and cooking and cleaning, and trying to give me undivided attention for long periods of time and conversation. I certainly appreciated (and still do) those things, but they did not and still do not make me feel loved.

So the first lesson for us was that our natural tendency is to express love in the way each of us most feels it, even when it may not feel loving to our spouse. I call this the love gap. We are trying to love but it may not be getting us completely there. We are not speaking the same language.

Second, that love gap meant that I needed to change. And so did Anita. We needed to discover and understand that we each needed something from the other that may not occur easily or naturally. I learned that in order for Anita to feel loved, I needed to stop, focus on her, and spend time each day in basic conversation. She loves that. And when possible, I needed to go out of my way to perform acts of service. When I do that, she receives and feels the love I want her to have from me. After all, she is my beautiful wife! God expects no less.

Likewise, Anita has learned that touching me and complimenting me are very important to my heart and soul. Just as I now make a conscious effort to speak and act in her love languages for her sake, she does the same for me.

And the result is a filling of our love banks. When I spend quality time or perform acts of service, I fill Anita's love bank. In the same way, her physical touch and encouraging words fill my bank.

Make no mistake: Couples enter the danger zone when the love bank is not being tended.

I still remember the sadness of those eyes. Dave and Melissa had been married about eight years. They lived on a farm and had three daughters. Melissa was beautiful—head-turning beautiful. When she went into town, men noticed.

Dave raised cattle, worked long, hard hours, and earned just enough to keep his family together in the small house they rented. His hours were long and unpredictable—no one can tell you when a cow will get sick or give birth. Dave was at work a lot, and when he was home, he was tired. There was precious little time or energy for listening, undivided attention, kindling the flames of relationship, or doing the hard work of maintaining emotional connection.

Melissa did most of the child rearing and home tending on her own. That is, until Dave got sick—so sick that he needed major surgery; so sick that his body could not recover and he had to take a leave of absence from work and the money ran out.

Melissa then went to work in a factory. She was doing her best, trying to keep the family intact. Stress was high. After all, her husband was sick, money was scarce, children get hungry, and the rent had to be paid. She soon found that in the factory she could escape all that pressure and stress. She was bright, a good worker, and beautiful. Her manager noticed. He took an interest in helping her to advance and also lent an attentive ear in which to confide. Not long after, he not only took an interest; he took advantage. Soon, the affair took over her life.

Dave was left in pain at home, with the children wondering where their mother was and desperation dripping out of the air vents of their lives.

Melissa tried to keep her marriage together. She didn't run away with her lover at first. That's why I remember the sadness of her eyes when she and Dave came to meet with me in a last-ditch effort to save their family. A few weeks later, she was gone.

Dave and Melissa are good people. He did his best. She gave it her all. But neither of them were able to tend to the love bank, and the account eventually became overdrawn.

So what do you do if your love bank is empty or running low?

Spend some time discovering what your mate's two primary love languages are and begin speaking those as generously as you possibly can. If your spouse feels loved when she receives gifts, make a plan to give her a simple gift several times a week. Not all gifts have to be purchased. A handwritten note or a flower thoughtfully picked from the yard can communicate love just as much as a bracelet or flowers bought at the store.

As you begin to love your mate more intentionally in a way he or she understands, chances are high that the love will flow back to you in return. When we feel loved, we usually share love generously. It's the law of the harvest. Beginning with an honest, caring conversation about love languages can prompt that.

Saint Paul is correct: If you want more love, begin giving more love away. And then watch as a harvest of love returns to you. Give what you wish to receive. And soon your love bank will begin to approach full. That is the secret of the love bank.

REAL-LIFE HELP

Spend five minutes sharing with your spouse the two love languages that are the most meaningful to you. Then listen as your spouse shares for five minutes in return. Do not comment or evaluate. Just listen.

To close the conversation, say together aloud, "Lord, teach us to love generously and to love well."

For additional help, I recommend Gary Chapman's book *The 5 Love Languages*, in which you can learn and study more about how to give and receive love in your marriage.

07

THE SECRET OF ROMANCE

Song of Songs is there for a reason.

Song of Songs may be the least read and most misunderstood book of the Bible. But this special book made the cut and became a part of the Bible for a reason.

God desires to be the lover of your soul. And Song of Songs makes that abundantly clear. In this little book of the Bible, you will discover the secret of romance.

The words of Solomon in the Song of Songs can be read at two levels. First, the poetry describes the relationship between a man and the woman he courts, with whom he then consummates his love. It is a love story. Second, that love describes the immense, passionate love God has for us humans, His created beings. The Divine yearns to romance our souls.

When you understand this simple truth, you begin to understand everything. God yearns to romance your soul.

Again, remember how the love of an earthly marriage is a reflection of the divine love that flows from God to us. In the best marriages, the love a husband shows for his wife reflects exactly how God feels for us. That's why the secret of romance is so very important. The love in your marriage can and should mirror the love God has for you.

Spend a moment absorbing the intense love of God and the romance that reflects it in a marriage in these words from the Song of Songs.

You have ravished my heart, my Sister, my Bride;
you have ravished my heart with one glance of your
eyes,
with one hair on your neck.

How beautiful are your breasts, my Sister, my Bride;
how much more delightful are your breasts than wine
and the fragrance of your ointments than all spices!

Sweetness drips from your lips, O Bride;
honey and milk are under your tongue,
and the scent of your robes is like the scent of Lebanon.

You are an enclosed garden, my Sister, my Bride,
an enclosed garden, a fountain sealed.
You are a park that puts forth pomegranates
with all choice fruits, with henna, with spikenard,

with nard and saffron, calamus and cinnamon, with
all the trees of Lebanon,
with myrrh and aloes and all the finest spices.
You are a garden fountain, a well of living water,
flowing fresh from Lebanon.

SONG OF SONGS 4:9-15
(TRANS.: FR. BASIL PENNINGTON, OCSO)

If your romance with your spouse is a reflection of our romance with our God, the stakes are high, aren't they? God's love for us pours like water out of the mountains and from the deserts, indeed from all creation. We are like choice fruits that God yearns to savor over and over again. Our souls capture God's heart, and in the same way, that soul captivation can lie at the heart of a marriage based in the faith.

God's love selflessly and generously creates us out of nothing. Out of love, He breathes into us the breath of life. He is the Lord, the giver of life. The love of God lives and stretches out from the arms of Jesus on the cross as He offers Himself for us and in our place. Jesus' eyes pierce our own as He gazes lovingly at us from the cross. In Jesus, God even suffers for us, His beloved.

Perhaps best of all, the love of God spills into our lives as He gives Himself to us fully in the Eucharist. In the very blood and body of Jesus present in the Eucharist, God places Himself in us, filling us with Himself. This is what Saint Bernard of Clairvaux calls the sacrament of endless union with God. A truly mystical union.

In fact, the entire Bible is a love story. Very simply, you are the beloved of the divine lover. You are cherished with a love beyond what human words can express. Let the streams of love invade you. God's love provides the base for the secret of romance.

As God loves you and me as His spouses, in the same way, a man loves a woman with delight. God's love gives the model for romance: selfless, sacrificial, and generous. Extravagant love.

By remembering Adam and Eve in the Garden, we realize "it is not good for man to be alone." (Genesis 2:18) Because we are made in God's own image, and therefore are filled with God's love, we are designed to give love away just as God does. We can love only through the sincere gift of ourselves. Sexual intimacy is meant to be an act of total self-giving, not all that different from God's self-giving in Jesus and in the Eucharist.

Saint John Paul II captured this well in his teaching and writing when he shared how God plans for sexuality to mirror His love for the world He created. His love for the world is one of openness to love and life, a life-giving relationship. The call to love as God loves is stamped in our very beings as male and female from the beginning. Our bodies do not make sense in isolation. They make sense only in communion with other people.

Adam desired to give. Eve's desire was to receive the gift and to give herself back. The gift of themselves to one another was free and sincere; hence there was no shame. That is God's plan for romance and sexuality in a marriage: generous self-giving.

Of course, romance and sex are not one and the same. As Anita humorously reminds me regarding sexual intimacy, women need a reason, while men just need a place. Remember that physical touch is often how men best give and receive love, while women prefer to be emotionally connected. As we learned in the secret of the love bank, talking and listening usually decreases a woman's stress level. Sexual intimacy happens when women are not stressed. Listening leads to emotional connection. That connection leads to touching.

Ultimately, the secret of romance needs to lie at the foundation of any thriving marriage.

Our culture has made sex into an idol, and ripped it from its intimate, loving home in a marriage. John Paul II reminded the Church that love does not include treating someone as merely an object of pleasure. But when we remember that God gives us the model and the plan for sex in a marriage and that romance is central to our love for each other and God's love for us, our love lives take on a whole new meaning. Sex unites a man and a woman physically, emotionally, and spiritually, in a way nothing else can. And love expressed through that self giving act also allows a husband and wife to partner with God in the creation of new life. We become co-creators with God. Like Eve said after birthing Cain, "I have produced a man with the help of the Lord." (Genesis 4:1)

This just keeps getting better, doesn't it? First, romance is at the heart of God's love for us. Second, our love for our mates is based on the same self-giving that Jesus models for us. Third, in sex, we can become co-creators with God, who made heaven and earth and all that is in them. Wow.

So what does all this mean for you and me as married people? Love will provide the foundation for marriage, just as it defines God's relationship with us. Romance helps keep that love alive and burning, just as the Eucharist and our spiritual lives with God keep love alive and burning. God's love flows passionately and continuously. And if our marriages are not only to survive but also to thrive, love will flow passionately and continuously in them as well.

Interestingly, a 1992 University of Chicago study even indicates that Christians, especially devout married Catholics, have the most satisfying sex lives of any demographic group. Those who attend worship together at least once a week have the highest sense of being loved in sexual intercourse, as do those couples who still have their first marriage intact. Contrary to pop culture opinion, faith and fidelity are integral to a satisfying sex life rather than detrimental. Song of Songs is correct.

Maintaining the secret of romance can be challenging. But with God generously giving His love to us, we have a deep reservoir to draw from to continue to find that romance and let it energize marriage.

REAL-LIFE HELP

Retell the story of how you and your spouse met and dated. Relive your courtship with the memories that only the two of you have. Spend time tonight sharing those stories again and giving thanks for the beginning of your romance. Your story is yours and yours alone. It is helpful every so often to share it aloud to keep the romance alive and well in your marriage. We hear the story of Jesus over and over again as a reminder of God's love. In the same way, hearing your spouse remember with gladness how you dated, courted, and married will kindle the flames of romance over and over again, because the two of you share something special. And that something special belongs only to you. Embrace your story. And embrace the secret of romance.

08

THE SECRET OF THE BEST FRIEND

_____

Don't marry someone you can live with; marry someone you can't live without.

The greatest piece of wisdom ever offered regarding marriage? It came from my grandmother. Whenever someone asked her about marriage, her first response always flowed out: "Don't marry someone you can live with; marry someone you can't live without." That's the secret of the best friend.

What does it mean? It means your marriage has its best shot if you marry your best friend. In a study by Robert and Jeanette Lauer of 351 successful couples with thriving marriages lasting longer than fifteen years, the top statement shared by those couples to describe their relationships was, "My spouse is my best friend."

We've already learned that romance lies at the heart of any thriving marriage. But that does not mean that you and your spouse will act like hormonal teenagers in goo-goo-eyed passion for the rest of your lives. It means there is a genuine attraction that lies underneath everything else in the relationship.

In fact, most relationships have a two-year sizzle period. That's the time when you can think of nothing other than your mate. You always remember that first kiss. Kissing is God's way of getting two people so close together that they cannot see what is wrong with each other. Sizzle. You are obsessed. It's two years during which the very sight of your partner quickens your pulse and you dream of nothing else. F. Scott Fitzgerald considered this sensation to be "a little like divine drunkenness." Sizzle.

But any mature human being knows that after a time, relationship sizzle calms down, and the reality of day-to-day living settles in. C. S. Lewis even wrote, "If the old fairy tale ending, 'They lived happily ever after' is taken to mean 'They felt for the next fifty years exactly as they felt the day before they were married,' then it says what probably never was nor ever could be true, and it would be highly undesirable if it were. Who could bear to live in that excitement for even five years? What would become of your work, your appetite, your sleep, your friendships? But of course, ceasing to 'be in love' need not mean ceasing to love."

Over time, this settling in is when authentic love either takes root or dies. At that moment, when the sizzle has subsided, every couple will make a decision to invest or to divest. To step in or step out. Each spouse will choose: Will I learn to love this person in ways deeper than emotional, heart pumping, star dreaming, or will I go in search of another two-year sizzle with someone else? If the answer is yes to a deeper love, the marriage and relationship will grow to a new level and increase its chances at thriving. If the answer is no, it will die a quick or sometimes slow and agonizing death. One or both partners will emotionally exit and begin looking for another pulse-quickening experience with someone else. They will have made the mistake of confusing lust for love.

Sam and Julie were married for more than fifty years. Each had a personality stronger than garlic. Opinions flowed. Heated debates abounded. But love thrived through rearing four children, being diagnosed with grave diseases, and enduring the ravages of old age. I will always remember meeting with Julie late in her life. Somehow the conversation turned to our culture's obsession with sex and the temptation to make marriage all about it, as if that were enough to build a life on. Julie volunteered to Anita and me, "Sex is nice, but it really has nothing to do with our marriage at this point. We have shared life together. We're sharing suffering together. Now we're looking toward the end of life together. Why would I want to do that with anyone else? Marriage has been so much larger than sex."

Julie may not have known it at the time, but she was describing the secret of the best friend. Long after the sizzle of a new relationship has cooled, a genuine and heartfelt friendship will ensure that you are able to build a life together.

Think about your closest friends in life and what you have had in common with them.

1) *Shared values: The same things matter to you*

2) *Shared interests: You enjoy the same kinds of activities*

3) *Trust in all things: You can count on that friend*

4) *Pleasure in being together: Delight and ease just sharing time*

5) *Occasions for confiding: A place for your deepest feelings and secrets*

If your marriage has these same qualities, expect it to thrive. Because these are the traits of the secret of the best friend.

Marriage is a partnership and a friendship more than anything else. As spouses building a life together over what you hope will be fifty years or more, you will mutually influence one another in all kinds of ways.

Remember again the story of Carlton and Maggie. When friends came to visit Carlton after Maggie died, his favorite topic was his late wife. They hadn't been just lovers. They had been sweethearts, deep friends, lifelong playmates. In other words, they knew the secret of the best friend.

In a similar way, Anita has been a wonderful influence in my life. It was Anita who helped reintroduce me to the faith when I had wandered a long way from God's designs for my life. She has had a marvelous impact on every ministry we've shared, and she has influenced my leadership with her spiritual maturity.

I had very little experience being around children when we first married. Through her remarkable mothering skills, Anita taught me how to be a good father. She has influenced my perspective on dozens of subjects because I respect her wisdom, value her opinion, and treasure her friendship. She is my best friend, and that is what has helped us move from surviving to thriving through some of the experiences I share in this book. She has influenced me. I have accepted and even embraced that influence. That's what best friends do.

In fact, John Gottman's work shows that 81 percent of marriages in which a man resists his wife's instruction will end in divorce. Some folks will say that is absurd, that a man needs to wear the pants, dig in his heels, stand firm and stand tall, that a man needs to call the shots and a woman just needs to submit to it. Others will hear this research and think it suggests a man should be a doormat or a jellyfish and acquiesce to any and all nagging: "Just do as she says."

However, this basic insight from Gottman's research applies not only to marriages but to all healthy relationships, whether with friends, coworkers, or siblings. Being stubborn and mulish is hardly the hallmark of a healthy person, nor are those traits good paths to strong relationships. Wise people seek input from others, listen to it, and then apply what is helpful. Receiving counsel and encouragement from people who care for you makes you stronger, not weaker.

The secret of the best friend will carry your marriage through the best times and the worst times. And the fact is, best friends influence each other, a lot. That's just what good friends do. If you show me a man who lets his wife speak truth into his life, I will show you a man whose marriage is thriving. After all, who doesn't desire a life partner who's looking out for our best interests, a mate who's seeking to help us become the-best-version-of-ourselves?

Show me a man who stubbornly refuses to let his wife influence him and I will show you a marriage looking for a lawyer. That's how big a difference emerges when you embrace the secret of the best friend.

REAL·LIFE HELP

Write a letter to your spouse. Share the parts of his or her personality and life that you love, admire, and respect the most. Give specific examples of times your spouse has enriched your life, stood by you as a best friend, spoken truth into you. Writing a letter gives you time to really think about what you want to say, just the way you want to say it. Take your time. Remind your spouse and yourself of the deep friendship that binds you together. Tell him or her, "You are my best friend." Embrace the secret of the best friend.

09

THE SECRET OF AGES AND STAGES

———

The only constant in your marriage will be the two of you and the fact you are changing as people and as a couple.

John and Amelia Rocchio, when they had been married eighty-two years, made the newspaper. They lived outside Providence, Rhode Island. He was 101; she was ninety-nine. At the time, their anniversary made them the longest-married couple in America. Asked what the secret to their longevity was, John answered, "Patience."

In that single word, John Rocchio captured the secret of ages and stages.

Imagine all the ages and stages their marriage had been through at that point. Here are just a few:

The sizzle of dating and the thrill of courtship and engagement.

The settling down of beginning a new life together as a married couple.

The transition to parenthood as children arrived.

The changing of roles as the children aged into adolescence and the parents became more like coaches than lifeguards.

The rediscovery of one another as mates when the nest emptied and John and Amelia were alone together again.

The celebration and welcoming of grandchildren and great-grandchildren.

The care giving as health issues and aging began to exact their toll.

The friendship of preparing to finish life well.

With so many phases in their relationship, it is easy to assume John and Amelia learned at least two things. First, marriages, like wine, grow, change, and mature over time. And second, that process in a marriage requires patience.

When you initially say, "I will love you for the rest of my life," the words flow easily and passionately from your lips. But then the rest of your life sets in, and you notice how your partner begins to change over time. Obviously, we physically change. I am still short, but there is nary a hair on my head and hasn't been since about the age of thirty-five. Anita didn't marry a bald man, but she has been married to one far longer than she was married to a man with fine hair.

We not only change physically. We also change in our tastes and preferences. I loved baseball as a young man, and now I do not care one whit about it. Our first date was to a baseball game. Now I would vastly prefer almost anything else, especially a visit to one of our favorite restaurants.

We change in our temperaments. Your spouse may grow more calm and mellow over time, or he or she may become more addled and anxious. Work may cause your spouse to lose some of the spark he had for life when he was younger. Or addiction may emerge in your mate and she will face struggles neither of you had ever anticipated.

Parenting will also change you. Health issues will change you. Suffering will change you. Your faith life will change you. The death of a close friend or your parent will change you. And the list goes on. You will change. That's a fact. You will change as a person, and so will your spouse. You will also have experiences together that change you as a couple.

How do you help your marriage not only survive, but thrive through all these inevitable changes? The secret of ages and stages. Or, in a word from the Rocchios, patience.

You will be experiencing these changes together. And the only constants will be the two of you and the fact that you are both changing. This process can be dizzying, frustrating, and even heart wrenching. As you observe your spouse changing over time, you may be reminded of the words of Walt Whitman in his poem "Song of Myself:"

Do I contradict myself?

Very well then, I contradict myself.

I am large. I contain multitudes.

But the point to remember is that change is not an option. Change will happen whether you like it or not. You will change, your spouse will change, and your relationship will evolve over time as a result.

It is tempting not to pay attention to the changes occurring in your spouse's life, soul, and priorities over time. After all, there are a lot of other areas of life that will require your attention, such as the daily survival and routines of work, home, children, finances.

It is even more tempting to pay attention only to the life changes you yourself are experiencing. Marketing researcher and author, Sheena Iyengar, captures this temptation: "I know myself in excruciating self-detail. I know what I think, feel, do every second I'm awake, and on the basis of this knowledge, I can confidently say that nobody else could possibly think, feel, do exactly the same . . . we regularly fail to recognize that others' thoughts and behaviors are just as complex and varied as our own."

The fact remains that you and your spouse will change over time, and that process requires attention. The goal is to share experiences and change together. But reality teaches that this is not easy.

When Maureen married Ken, she knew he was an alcoholic. However, she loved him and had always been able to find ways to cope with his addiction during their dating. Plus, she figured, she would pray for him each day and hope one day God would lead him into sober recovery.

For fifteen years, through the birth of four children, Maureen prayed diligently for Ken to overcome his alcoholism. She grew accustomed to managing life and family without Ken's full or healthy participation. Remarkably, their marriage managed to survive in spite of his addiction.

Finally, after their fifteenth anniversary, Ken expressed his desire to get clean and sober once and for all. Maureen rejoiced in the news.

Unlike in his previous efforts, this time Ken kept his word. He got help, he found a counselor, he regularly attended Alcoholics Anonymous meetings, and with God's help, he moved his life into recovery. During his first year of sobriety, the children adjusted to having a more stable father. Home life began to change.

But Maureen did not adjust. Eighteen months after Ken's move to sobriety, he and Maureen divorced. In short, she knew how to date, marry, and live with an alcoholic man. She could not figure out how to be married to a sober one. Ken had changed. Maureen had not.

Change is hard. When the grace of God is involved in that change, the process becomes even more difficult. Flannery O'Connor's wise words ring true: "All human nature vigorously resists grace because grace changes us and change is painful."

So how do you embrace the change that will occur in each of you and in your marriage, especially when that change is painful?

To change together requires courage and patience. Acceptance and grace must prevail. But remember, as your partner is changing, so are you. This is a two-way street, and one that must be traveled together. When a couple tells me they have "grown apart," I know that they have not changed together. Patience has been absent. Demands have been many, and grace has left the building.

Patience originates in the Holy Spirit Himself. And you begin to live in the Holy Spirit the moment you are baptized. In the first-century Church, men and women stripped naked as they entered the baptismal pool, symbolizing how they were taking off the old self. When they emerged from the baptism, they clothed themselves in a white robe, symbolizing the new self in Christ. When you are becoming the-best-version-of-yourself, you clothe yourself with patience. That is possible only because of your baptism, when you put on Christ.

And patience means learning to be patient with other people, even to the point of forgiveness. In other words, just as God is patient with you and your failures, so too does He desire that you will be patient with your spouse. You must bear with one another even when shortcomings and failures are apparent.

Peter's example is a good place to start. Think of Jesus' relationship with the man who would become Saint Peter. In this one relationship alone, Jesus demonstrates how patience, bearing with one another in love, and forgiveness are all linked together. Remember how:

1) *Jesus calls Peter to leave his fishing business and "follow" Him to become a fisher of men. Peter obeys Jesus immediately. (Mark 1:16–20)*

2) *Peter is a witness as his own mother-in-law is healed by Jesus. (Mark 1:29–31)*

3) Peter witnesses firsthand the remarkable life of Jesus as Jesus heals the sick, feeds the multitudes, teaches the crowds, and rebukes the Pharisees. Jesus routinely invests significant time and energy in Peter.

4) Peter confesses that Jesus is the Messiah when Jesus asks, "Who do you say that I am?" He clearly has been paying attention and knows Jesus well. Peter knows who Jesus is. (Mark 8:27–30)

5) In spite of the fact that Peter knows who Jesus is, he rebukes Jesus for teaching the disciples that the Son of Man must die and rise again. Hear that: Peter rebukes Jesus. Maybe he doesn't get it as much as we thought he did. In turn, Jesus rebukes Peter with the famous words, "Get behind me, Satan. You are not thinking as God does, but as human beings do." (Mark 8:31–33)

6) Peter then witnesses Jesus' transfiguration on the mountain when Elijah and Moses appear. He even suggests that booths be built so that everyone can stay on top of the mountain rather than returning to their mundane lives. (Mark 9:2–8)

7) Peter is present when Jesus enters Jerusalem, cleanses the temple, and instructs His followers about the coming crucifixion and the end times. He shares in the Lord's Supper in the upper room when Jesus eats with his disciples for the final time. (Mark 14:12–25)

8) Jesus tells Peter that he will be the one disciple to deny Him. Peter rejects these words and even says that he is willing to go to death with Jesus. Knowing

full well that Peter will fail, Jesus is nevertheless patient with his braggadocio. (Mark 14:27–31)

9) *Jesus is patient with Peter even as he falls asleep in the Garden of Gethsemane while Jesus prepares to die. In spite of simple instructions to stay awake, Peter has to be awakened by Jesus three separate times. (Mark 14:32–42)*

10) *As the end nears, Peter publicly denies Jesus not once but three times. (Mark 14:66–72)*

11) *Finally, Peter is nowhere to be found as Jesus is crucified, dies, and is buried. (Mark 15:33–16:8)*

What is the point of all this? Very simple: Peter ebbs and flows. He changes a lot. Like most humans do.

Peter shows signs of greatness as he leads the disciples. He shows remarkable weakness as he fails Jesus and even denies Him. He shows great insight by knowing and understanding who Jesus is. Yet he shows a huge gap in understanding by telling Jesus that the Son of Man should not suffer and die. Remarkably, Jesus stands by Peter. He does not give up on Peter or cast him out of the followers. He is patient as Peter ebbs and flows. Jesus is constant; He is patient. Always, even to the end. Because God is patient.

Even when Jesus knows that Peter will deny Him, still He takes Peter along to the Garden of Gethsemane. Still He is patient with Peter. And when Peter is broken down and seemingly lost after denying Jesus three times, the risen Jesus returns to make a special appearance to him.

To the very end, Jesus is patient with Peter. Most stunningly of all, Jesus restores Peter to the leadership role among the followers. Jesus is patient time and again with him. Even when Peter has seemingly dropped the ball in the worst way, Jesus has the last word. And that word is redemption.

When Peter falters or stumbles, still Jesus is there. When Peter rebukes or denies Jesus, still Jesus bears with him in love. And in the end, Jesus forgives Peter, the ultimate example of patience, bearing with one another in love, and forgiveness.

Being patient with your husband day after day, year after year, is not a natural human thing to do. Being patient with your wife as she changes in small ways or large requires a lot. You cannot do these things without the Spirit of God assisting you in your life. However, with the Spirit, you cannot help but grow more patient and forgiving with all of these people in your life. It will happen. Why? Because God is patient. The very same remarkable patience that God showed with Peter, He will share with you.

Nevertheless, growing and changing with your spouse requires two things: patience and communication. Remember the secret of purpose. You are helping your spouse get to heaven and display the traits God desires. "Love, joy, peace, *patience*," reads the list from Saint Paul in Galatians. In Ephesians 4:1–2, Saint Paul says, "I . . . urge you to live in a manner worthy of the call you have received, with all humility and gentleness, *with patience, bearing with one another through love.*" Patience is part of the Kingdom of God. God is patient, and you will grow in patience if you are growing in God. As you grow in patience with your mate, he or she will thrive. And the result will likely be more patience with you.

Patience enables you to endure change. In fact, it allows you to thrive through change because you know that your spouse is always changing and your relationship is always evolving. The ages and stages of marriage become something you anticipate rather than dread. Patience helps you look eagerly ahead to what God will do next rather than resenting that your spouse has added a few pounds here and there or no longer likes to go camping like she used to.

Communication is the first cousin of patience. The love language of quality time hinges on listening attentively to your spouse each day. When that listening occurs, you will quickly discover that you know firsthand how your mate is feeling, growing, and changing. Surprises will occur less frequently because you will know your partner well and see those changes coming. And when you know and can anticipate change, patience becomes much easier.

On my forty-fourth birthday, I became Catholic. Flannery O'Connor said, "You don't join the Catholic Church. You become Catholic." Since I had been serving as senior pastor of a Protestant megachurch, that change obviously created some waves in our lives as a couple and as a family. (Details on that decision are fully shared in my book *Confessions of a Mega Church Pastor: How I Discovered the Hidden Treasures of the Catholic Church*.)

However, that transition in my life caused very little turbulence in our marriage. For nearly fifteen years, I had been sharing with Anita the questions, struggles, experiences, and thoughts I was having in my faith life. She had been clued in along the way. She was very much a part of the journey. We were traveling together. Communication had helped prepare her for that major change. Communication produced patience, and patience navigated us through a new age and stage in our relationship when I converted.

Naturally, Anita and I were the subjects of criticism, misinformation, and rumors when I came into the Church. After all, I was leaving behind a long ministry in the Protestant world, and some people in our lives did not understand or appreciate the journey or the decisions I was making. Anita and I were able to take in stride crazy rumors (that we were getting a divorce, or I had done something untoward) because we had good communication habits established over the twenty years of our marriage. Because we had routinely shared our feelings and thoughts in long, intimate conversations, Anita was not shocked when I made the transition, nor were we concerned about what others might suggest. We knew the truth and had shared it with each other often.

On the other hand, I had not done as good a job in communicating some of those same experiences and thoughts to my children over the years, so my transition caused more turbulence in their lives than I would have desired. If I could do that over again, I would rethink it, because communication leads to patience. And patience leads to hope. And hope will propel your marriage and relationships forward through change and often cause them to thrive in the process.

Patience and communication will make the difference between aging together and growing apart.

Finally, our culture has moved toward older ages for first marriages. On average, men now are about thirty when they marry for the first time, and women are twenty-seven or twenty-eight. I swim strongly against the culture in this debate. When you marry younger (not in your teens, but in your early to mid-twenties), you have fewer ingrained habits and ways of doing things. You have not fully established your own independent, individual life. As a result, you are more open to change. And marriage brings change.

Marrying younger allows you to grow up together, as long as you have the basic secrets of friendship and purpose in place. Growing up together as a couple will give you more experiences to base your relationship on and will also allow you to merge together before so many patterns in your life are set in concrete. In other words, marrying younger will prepare you to change together over the course of the rest of your lives, because you will have been changing together all along the way. One observer has compared this to being a business start-up, in which everything is new, as opposed to a business merger, in which two long-standing entities come together with their own histories, habits, and behaviors. Marrying later will likely require some jackhammer removal of concrete in your life as you adjust to being with a second person with his or her own way of doing things.

When I read about the Rocchios on their eighty-second wedding anniversary, it reminded me of attending a seventieth wedding anniversary celebration. At the reception, I spoke to the couple and asked them the secret of being married for seventy years. (As you can tell, I've always been interested in this theme!) The woman looked at me and said, "Neither one of us died."

She may well be right. Long marriages may simply be the result of just living a long time. But you and I know that patience helped this couple along the way.

Saint Teresa of Ávila was right: Patience achieves everything, through the secret of ages and stages.

REAL-LIFE HELP

Spend some time today talking about the ages and stages of your relationship. What stages have you completed? What are some of your favorite memories from each of those? What stage do you think you are in now? What is the greatest challenge of this particular stage or age for you as a person or as a couple?

Conclude the conversation by imagining together what you both would desire your life to look like when you celebrate your fiftieth wedding anniversary. Remember the core priority you wrote down after chapter 1.

Where will you be living on your fiftieth anniversary? How would you like to honor that celebration? What kinds of memories do you hope to have then? Form a picture in your mind so that the two of you visualize your future together. Sharing that mental picture will guide you through the ages and stages to come.

Mental simulation works because we can't imagine events or sequences without stimulating the same parts of the brain that are touched in real life. Such visualization helps us manage emotions and can help us create the future we desire.

Mental simulation can even build life skills, so envision together what you want your relationship to be like. And this visualization will help prepare you for the ages and stages still to come.

10

THE SECRET OF THE BED

---

*If being together bothers you, your marriage
has entered the danger zone.*

Nearly one in four American married couples no longer share
a bed. Home builders report a growing increase in requests
for separate master bedroom suites and expect such requests
eventually to become the norm for new homes. Sometimes that
is for health reasons such as sleep apnea, snoring, or restless legs.
At other times it is another step to help the marriage survive. As
the comedian Rodney Dangerfield liked to say, "We're sleeping
in separate bedrooms. We take separate vacations. We have

separate checking accounts. We're doing everything we can to keep this marriage together."

Flying in the face of these facts is the secret of the bed. We can all agree that sometimes sleeping separately is necessary. In the same way, all of us should agree that it is not optimal. Acceptable is not the same as *desirable*. *OK* is not the same as best. The secret of the bed is more important than we know. And, to be honest, it is a profound mystery.

There is a difference between merely surviving and really thriving. You are likely reading this book because you know that God created us males and females for each other, and that a marriage binds two people together as one for a lifetime. Marriage creates a special bond, a unique union. God is at work in marriage in a way that is unlike in any other relationship, creating a mystical union that is dynamic and morphing.

Nothing embodies that mystical union like the marriage bed. I am not talking about sex here. Rather, this secret is all about intimacy. And it is a mystery just like the marital union itself.

Somehow, as the two become one, there is something unique and special about sharing a bed. It is more than a physical closeness. Pillow talk, gentle touches, and occasional tugs-of-war over the sheets all occur. And so does intimacy—deep, growing intimacy that can develop only one evening at a time, week after week, over the course of years.

I recently spent some time with an older friend, Jill. She lives by herself now, and we had not seen each other for several years. Her husband had suffered for years from a chronic debilitating illness. In his last few months, he was moved into a nursing facility for around-the-clock care. Each day, Jill would sit with him in his room for most of the day, visiting while he was awake, knitting when he slept.

While we were chatting, I asked Jill about caring for her husband for so many years and what stood out in her mind about her noble service to him as he died. She replied, "I think he knew he was going to die on the day he did. I sat with him in his room and we were reminiscing about our fifty years of marriage. He looked at me and asked, 'Honey, will you just lie next to me in the bed here for a few minutes?' So I got in the nursing home bed alongside him, and we held each other for a little while.

"We reminisced about the first bed we shared after our marriage. It was just a twin bed. And we laughed and remembered that tiny bed and those days so long ago. I got out of the nursing home bed and went home that evening.

"About two o'clock in the morning, the nursing home called to share with me that he had had a heart attack and died. I think he knew the end was near. I think that's why he wanted just to lie next to each other in the bed one last time. Just to share that closeness."

Jill's precious memory stirred something deep about the dignity and meaning of a marriage that lasts a lifetime, one filled with highs and lows but rooted in a deep love, friendship, and affection for one another and for God. In a way, the final experience she and her husband shared captures the very spirit of Hebrews 13:4: "Let marriage be honored among all and the marriage bed be kept undefiled . . ."

Here's to a marriage well done and what it teaches the rest of us about fidelity, love, and virtue.

It really is hard to describe. There's a mystical and sacred element to that shared space where something as personal as sleep, bad breath, and yes, even lovemaking occurs.

Anita and I graduated to a queen-size bed several years ago. We'd been in a double bed for the first twenty years of our marriage. I liked that double bed. I enjoyed bouncing off each other, an elbow here, a knee there, our bodies tangled together. A certain closeness, a unity, develops from that, one that cannot happen any other way. I feel oddly connected, in the loop, integrated with my wife. One.

Sharing that bed also helps our conflict resolution. I am a pouter. It's not a good trait, and Anita has spent many years trying to help me unlearn that bad habit. She likes to reconcile and iron out anything before we go to sleep. She reminds me often, "Do not let the sun set on your anger, and do not leave room for the devil." (Ephesians 4:26–27) Sharing a bed forces the issue. I have to express myself because I am lying right next to her. The bed leaves me no choice.

You get the point. If one spouse is always wanting more personal time for herself, time with his own friends, space for her own vacation, his own bedroom, the marriage is trending in the wrong direction. If being together bothers you, your marriage is entering the danger zone. In much the same way, when the husband is using alcohol or narcotics to numb himself, it often signals that the marriage is in trouble, because he no longer enjoys being fully present with his wife. He's using substances to create some distance. Not desiring to share a bed often signals a similar lack of pleasure in simply being together.

When marriage bonds begin to erode, a number of red flags arise. What to many is a seemingly small thing, like no longer sharing the same bed, often indicates deeper issues. The sense of intimacy and trust may well be breaking down. When intimacy and trust begin to disappear, the couple no longer finds satisfaction or comfort in the simple act of being together.

In the same way, we often find it hard to see the unhealthy patterns that have crept into our relationship and behaviors. Remember the secret of the little things. When small negative interactions outnumber positive ones, a marriage's vital signs are flashing warnings to the husband and wife, whether they see them or not. The biggest warning signs are the destructive communication habits (the four horsemen of the apocalypse): criticism, contempt, stonewalling, and defensiveness. When these habits become routine, the apocalyptic end of a marriage becomes much more likely. A couple may not notice, but these four horsemen are wreaking havoc at the deep levels of trust and intimacy that undergird the marriage.

Criticism and defensiveness may initially seem like smaller things, but they are indicators of a deeper crisis in the making. Often, that is true also for the secret of the bed. Choosing to sleep in separate beds may seem small and insignificant at the time, but it often points to a deeper divide that has developed in the marriage.

The secret of the bed is a mystery. Then again, so is marriage. The sacraments are a mystery too, but God shows up every single time. Of course, God is a mystery too, isn't He? And our God designed us for intimacy—the intimacy of the sacraments with

Him, and the intimacy that the shared marital bed provides a couple in its own remarkable way.

REAL·LIFE HELP

Lie on the bed together as a couple. Do not touch each other. Say nothing. Just look each other in the eyes. Do this for three full minutes, eye-to-eye, next to each other, on the bed. You are re-establishing a deeper bond.

Build this simple practice into your life as a couple several times a year. And the mystery of the secret of the bed will begin to find its way into you.

"For man is created in the image and likeness of God who is himself love. Since God created him man and woman, their mutual love becomes an image of the absolute and unfailing love with which God loves man."

CATECHISM OF THE CATHOLIC CHURCH 1604

IV. CRUCIAL SECRETS

"Cast yourself upon God and have no fear."

SAINT AUGUSTINE

11

THE SECRET OF PRIORITIES

Every marriage will face a turning point.

Life is about priorities. Love is about priorities. And a marriage thrives when it embraces the secret of priorities.

Show me your calendar or phone and I'll show you your priorities. When you make time for something, it becomes your priority. Where you invest your time is where you are investing yourself. Show me your bank statement and I'll show you your priorities. When you spend money or give money, your heart becomes attached and that project or item becomes a priority.

After all, Jesus said, "Where your treasure is, your heart will follow."(Matthew 6:21) Your heart follows your money.

When I was sixteen, I desperately pined for a car. I asked my dad if I could have a car. He said, "Sure, son, just as soon as you figure out how to pay for it." So I went to work. I decided not to play baseball in high school so I could work to afford a car. Purchasing that car became my priority. I organized my life around it. Finally, after lots of hard work, I had saved enough to buy myself a very used Volkswagen Rabbit. It was a bit rusty, but it ran. It leaked, so I had rainwater in my back floorboard whenever the storms came. Girls certainly were impressed by that unintentional foot-washing device. But it was my car. I owned it. I had purchased it with my own money. I bought the gas and paid for the upkeep.

After buying that car in high school, I spent most Saturdays washing that jalopy. I became expert at painstakingly creating the greatest luster and shine on the old green Rabbit. I spent still more time applying Armor All to the tires and to the interior of the car so they sparkled. That car became my priority. In order to say yes to that car, I said no to baseball, I said no to trips to the beach with friends, I said no to anything that would consume money or time that I needed for my car. The car was my priority. That's where my time and my money went.

When your priorities change, your life changes in the same direction.

I was enamored of that car for several years, until my interest cooled a bit. I found other things that were more interesting to me, like girls. They also required money and time. My priorities changed. And how I used my time and my money changed.

Eventually, I moved on to another car, and then another. I barely remember that first car now. It was my priority for a while, but things changed. Life moved on. I developed new priorities—because after all, it was only a car, right?

You get the point. If getting a new job is your priority, you will spend time getting the education and experience you need, and networking to make the contacts necessary to acquire that new job. That's your priority.

If recreation is your priority, you will allocate free time in your schedule for that extra round of golf or to spend time at the lake. You will adjust your budget to trim other costs so that more money is available for your recreational pleasure.

When your priorities change, your life changes in the same direction. When your relationship and marriage are your priority, then you will adjust your time and your money to reflect that. Some couples start off with the priority like I had with my first car. They spend all their time together, and they spend most of their money together. But eventually the interest cools. He may find himself investing more time in golf and his poker buddies. She may have outlets with her friends at work or in the neighborhood. Slowly, the couple begins merely to coexist. A slight distance sets in. That distance grows slowly but surely each year, sometimes peacefully, sometimes not so much, for the rest of the relationship.

However, you and I believe that God has created marriage for most of us as the primary way by which we will be transformed into the-best-version-of-ourselves—our holiest, most saintly selves. And we believe that God's love is made known to us in powerful ways in our marriage when we allow it to happen. If you believe these things are true, your marriage will be your priority for the rest of your days. Should your priorities change, expect real shifts to occur in your marriage. That is the secret of priorities.

One word the Church uses to capture the secret of priorities is *covenant*. God initiates a covenant. God's covenant revolves around His steadfast and exclusive love for His people. God is faithful and His covenant is unbreakable. It is a commitment, and it is God's priority. We base marriage on that example.

God's covenant begins in the Old Testament with His relationship with His chosen people of Israel. He initiates that covenant with Abraham and then with Moses. "I will be your God, and you will be my people." (Exodus 19:5ff)

Israel strays from God and disobeys Him time and time again. Nevertheless, God still remains faithful to His promises. He continues to call His people back to Himself. His covenant is unbreakable, and God will be faithful.

Jeremiah captures God's never-failing love and persistence when he writes what God told him: "'This is the covenant I will make with the house of Israel after that time,' declares the Lord. 'I will put my law in their minds and write it on their hearts. I will be their God and they will be my people. . . . I will forgive their wickedness and remember their sins no more.'" (Jeremiah 31:33–34)

This is a God for whom the covenant is a priority. He does not waver. He continues to pursue and to love.

Finally, God extends that covenant to the entire world in Jesus. His love and faithfulness are no longer focused only on Israel. As Jesus eats with His disciples for the last time in the upper room, He shares, "This cup is the new covenant in my blood, which is poured out for you." (Luke 22:20)

When God describes a covenant, He is not thinking about a simple contract or an agreement to hang out together as long as both He and we enjoy it. God's covenant involves unwavering love expressed in the sacrifice of His own Son, who is willing to die in order to bring us home. That covenant includes regular nourishment in the Eucharist and regular communication in prayer. Now that covenant is a priority.

Similarly, the Church teaches that marriage is a covenant. A covenant is unbreakable. And covenants take priority. That is one of the reasons why couples who live together before they marry are far more likely not to marry at all, and if they do, they are more likely to divorce than couples who do not live together. The "test drive" argument does not work because living together lacks the very heart of a covenant marriage. You do not stumble or ease into a marriage. Rather, you make a deep commitment. Priority.

Marriage may be the last modern institution based on covenant, and even that appears to be an endangered species in our culture now. We humans like convenience and disposability far more than we do covenants and unbreakable promises that are reliably and honorably kept. But deep down, you and I know what is good for us. Actually, we know what is best for us. We are at our best when we are faithful rather than reckless. We become more holy when we keep our promises rather than break them. We are most proud when we persist rather than quit. And we are most joyful when we are fully loving and being loved rather than always looking for the next good thing, which usually turns out to be as unsatisfying as the last thing or relationship we tried.

God's idea of a covenant is an unbreakable, everlasting commitment, a nonnegotiable promise. That concept came to my mind several years ago when I walked into a funeral home to visit one of my friends whose grandmother had died. As I entered the parlor, I saw the grandmother's body lying in the casket. Next to the casket sat her husband, my friend's grandfather, in his wheelchair. He had lifted her arm from the casket in order to hold her hand as he greeted the handful of visitors stopping by to offer him comfort. From his wheelchair, he gently caressed her hand and mentioned to each visitor that he and she had been just a few days shy of their sixtieth anniversary when she died. Years ago, he had made a nonnegotiable promise. *For better, for worse, until death do us part.* Covenant.

That is what God has in mind because it leads us to be our best selves. The marriage covenant does not shackle us. Just the opposite—it frees us to realize our full potential. The covenant unleashes a new dimension of love.

In that way, perception determines behavior. When you perceive marriage as a covenant created by God, unbreakable and everlasting, that perception changes your behavior. Your marital covenant takes priority. You invest yourself and your resources in this special promise. And that new behavior creates destiny. You will discover new portions of yourself and your own capacity to grow and love because you have committed yourself to this divinely ordained covenant. You will move toward the-best-version-of-yourself through this covenant as you and your spouse help each other get to heaven. Perception determines behavior. Behavior then determines destiny.

Focusing on what God has in mind pays far more dividends in life than focusing merely on what I might want at any given moment. After all, at one moment when I was younger, I let my heart get attached to an old, rusty car. That is why the Church teaches that marriage is a covenant.

Covenants take priority. Priorities require time, they require effort, and they usually require money. Best of all, marriages are worth every bit of it. That is the secret of priorities.

REAL-LIFE HELP

In Isaiah 54:10, God says to Israel, His covenant people: "Though the mountains be shaken and the hills be removed, yet my unfailing love for you will not be shaken nor my *covenant* of peace be removed."

These words capture just how much of a priority the covenant with His people is for God. They also apply to the covenant of marriage. As a couple, take turns reading this verse aloud to each other. It will reinforce the strength and beauty of covenant in your marriage.

When you have each done that, spend some time looking at your calendar for this week. Do not look back or too far ahead. Look at this week only. A mere seven days. Are there places where how you use your daily time reflects just how great a priority your marriage and family are for you as a couple? Are there changes or adjustments that the two of you need to make in this week's schedule to be sure that your best self is coming out for your marriage? Discuss this together and sketch out what the coming seven days might hold.

After discussing these questions, read Isaiah 54:10 to each other one more time. Give thanks to God for the covenant of your marriage and for His faithfulness to you and His people.

12

THE SECRET OF SEPARATION

Cleaving means cleaving.

Mother-in-law. The word itself often sends chills down your spouse's spine. Men worry about the nagging or meddling that can come from a mother-in-law. Women worry about the behind-the-scenes controlling that often is associated with the mother-in-law.

What's the solution? The secret of separation.

Look again at the words of Jesus when He describes marriage: "But from the beginning of creation, God made them male and female. *For this reason a man shall leave his mother and father and be joined to his wife*, and the two shall become one flesh. So they are no longer two but one flesh. Therefore what God has joined together, *no human being must separate*." (Mark 10:6–9)

You already know from the secret of synergy how the two become one. But notice how Jesus specifically mentions a man separating from his mother and father in order to form his own family. In this translation, the goal is to "join to" his wife. Older translations use the word *cleave*. In other words, "a man shall leave his mother and father and cleave to his wife."

Cleave. There's a word you don't hear much anymore. What in the world does it mean? It means to adhere. To stick closely to. To remain faithful. In other words, cleaving is like clinging, but with an especially passionate intensity. You cleave to a life buoy. You cleave to a friend the last time you see him before he goes off to war.

When cleaving occurs, two things (or in this case two people) combine so intensely that it is almost impossible to separate them. They are passionately connected to each other. They are not merely roommates or friends of convenience.

These words are important for a marriage to prosper. Cleaving matters.

When a plant is in a small pot and a seed falls from it to begin a new plant, what happens? There's not enough room in the single small pot for the second plant to really grow or thrive. It gets crowded out by the parent plant.

In the same way, for a marriage to really thrive, it must stand on its own. If either set of in-laws meddles, hovers, and controls, the new marriage will struggle to stand on its own. Either the man did not fully leave his mother and father, or the woman's parents are preventing him from truly cleaving to his new wife. In either example, the new marriage will be weak and dependent rather than strong and fully independent.

That's the secret of separation. A man and wife must separate themselves from their families in order for their new marriage and family to grow into all it can be. Separation may mean physical or geographic separation. Living with your in-laws or in their backyard can make it difficult to cleave and form your own identity as a couple.

Many couples find it necessary to live with or very near their families for financial reasons, or to provide child care or elder care. This arrangement can bear many dividends, particularly when the couple has been married for a number of years before moving into the multigenerational setting. However, in the case of newlyweds, the young couple will usually encounter some challenges in forming their own bond independent of the parents' involvement.

That does not make the situation impossible. It may mean having some honest conversations about boundaries and writing some of those down so that everyone can be reminded of them on occasion. It may require finding times to be separated from the parents, perhaps in the decision about which church to attend, where to eat certain meals, or how to spend free time, so that the couple can find environments that belong uniquely to them without interference.

Separation may also mean an emotional separation. If one person has an emotional overdependence on a parent, usually the mother, that will inhibit full emotional attachment to the new spouse.

The reverse can also prove true. For Ron and Vicky, the challenges came not from being too dependent on parents and family but from having no real family to learn from or provide a base of stability and love. As we did their premarital counseling together, we shared a conversation about family history and what each spouse would be bringing to the marriage. Most couples tend to create the marriage they have seen and grown up in.

That was a concern for Ron. He shared that his mother had been married three times and he had never met his father. He told of his own first marriage and divorce and the collateral damage done to the two children from the breakup. He felt so alone in the world that when I asked him about what habits he would be bringing to the marriage from his family, the Wilsons, he said, "I am the Wilson family."

For Ron, learning to cleave would be welcomed but challenging. He yearned to have that kind of relationship with his wife, yet he had experienced brokenness and disappointment in every familial relationship he'd ever had. For him, his family of origin would not be meddling; they would be completely absent, except for the pain they had left behind in his life. For him, cleaving would be a new concept. He would need to create new habits in order to learn how to cleave in a healthy way to his new wife, Vicky.

Separation can be created in several ways, and may occasionally even need to include counseling to help the spouses see the overdependence that limits their own growth as a unified whole. Sometimes, that needed separation naturally occurs when the new couple goes through an emotional crisis together and comes out on the other side to find themselves more fully merged and independent. Nothing has the potential to produce cleaving for a couple like sharing a period of intense suffering.

Anita and I experienced the secret of separation in several of these ways. A few years after we married, we moved to New Haven, Connecticut. We moved so that I could pursue a Ph.D. in New Testament and Ancient Christian Origins at Yale. It was a terrific opportunity, but it also meant relocating a thousand miles away from Georgia, our home, and a thousand miles away from any of our relatives. While that was not always easy for us, given that we had two children under the age of two when we moved, it also presented a marvelous chance for ours to become a full, independent marriage ready to thrive.

However, that journey was not easy. It was powerful and effective, but it was not easy, probably because for the first time we also learned to suffer together. And nothing tests a marriage for good or ill like suffering together. Our time in New Haven placed our marriage and our young family in a crucible of suffering that would make us or break us.

Suffering changes things. I do not know why. I do not invite it. I certainly do not encourage it in my own life. I rarely meet anyone who asks God to send more suffering. Yet somehow through the Holy Spirit, time and again, the hand of God uses the worst times in my life to grow my spirit and to bring about growth in ways that could not occur otherwise. The deepest lessons for marriage often come through the University of Hard Knocks. Some things simply cannot be learned in a book. Some things you will learn only when you live them.

Simply put, our time in New Haven was the worst three years of our life as a couple. They also proved to be three of the most wonderful years. That is how suffering works.

Up to that point, Anita and I had lived fairly easy lives, to be honest. During those years, my body was afflicted with an intense chronic case of ulcerative colitis, which we and our doctors were never able to get under control, not even with experimental treatments and megadoses of steroids. It caused me to spend several hours each day in the bathroom writhing in pain and bleeding, as I watched my body shed thirty pounds. That physical suffering took its toll on my mind and spirit, on our children, and on our marriage. I became increasingly difficult to live with due to the steroids making my fuse much shorter and my personality more volatile than it normally was. Anita learned to walk on eggshells around me and to protect the girls from the unpredictability of my moods. When we went places together as a family, we had to plan each step of the way to know where every public restroom was and how quickly I could get there in case of an emergency. And the emergencies came fairly often, and occasionally ended in embarrassing messes. Our life together was fragile.

The strain ultimately resulted in my having my entire colon and large intestine removed and replaced by a bag that I will wear on my body each day for the rest of my life, a simple reminder of the battle.

During these three years, Anita also suffered two miscarriages. In fact, there was one day when both of us lay in beds in the same hospital, just doors apart, undergoing medical procedures while a caring relative came from a thousand miles away to take care of our girls. We had never felt so helpless.

Things only got worse a few months later when a doctor diagnosed me with an early case of melanoma, the skin cancer that kills. Fortunately, that diagnosis came early enough that the treatments could provide a cure.

It is hard to describe—hard to imagine, really—but somehow, through this period of being isolated from our families while enduring a crucible of physical suffering, we each experienced the hand of God in a new and vital way.

Through the love and assurance of friends in our new town, through the prayers of other believers scattered around the globe, and through the presence of the Holy Spirit in our darkest hours, somehow we both grew closer to God and to each other. Remarkably, God worked in this suffering to rearrange my priorities and help me to see what is truly of value in this lifetime. A number of things that I had previously hoped to do in my life and my ministry suddenly fell by the wayside. I realized that God had clearly given me the mission of sharing the Good News about Jesus and that many other things in my life were distractions from that calling.

I no longer knew for sure how long I might live; God made it quite clear to me that time is of the essence and a sense of urgency can be a good thing. In the face of death, I learned a healthy impatience for the things of life that simply do not matter. More important, as a couple, Anita and I learned to be patient when things looked dark or bleak. God is still in control, and we learned to trust Him.

Doctors could not help; family could not help; my education could not help; our dreams and goals could not help. Only God could be our help and our hope. He taught us that patience. Without suffering, we likely never would have learned that.

As a result, Anita and I emerged from that trial of suffering bonded together in a powerful way. We certainly did not realize it at the time, but those three years caused us to separate from our families and to stand completely on our own. And that standing prepared us for the next twenty-five years of our life together. We shared experiences, both good and bad, that no one else was a part of. We had our own unique history, stories and feelings that only we knew, and from that, God generated a strength that has endured ever since.

In short, our time in New Haven helped us to cleave to one another and to God. And that is God's design. For a couple to thrive, the secret of separation will bring a necessary power and strength.

REAL-LIFE HELP

Suffering together as a couple often helps or accelerates the separation and cleaving process. Sometimes we experience God's presence most when we are suffering, and sometimes couples experience the depth of their love for one another during a time of great struggle.

Take a moment to think over the life of your relationship, whether it is a few months or many decades old. Remember a time when you experienced a challenge, a crisis, or a time of suffering together. Share with each other what you felt then and what you have learned from that experience. Has it brought you closer together as a couple? In what ways? How is your relationship different because of that time? How do you cleave to one another now?

If you are struggling to cleave together, discuss some of the reasons you think that may be the case. Do not try to solve the entire issue in one conversation. Listen attentively to one another and make a promise to continue the conversation in the coming days and weeks.

After spending a few minutes discussing this topic, hold hands and say a short prayer together. If time permits, you might want to try the Dynamic Catholic Prayer Process (see chapter 4). It provides a simple, helpful way for you to pray together as a couple.

13

THE SECRET OF INSIDERS

When in doubt, turn toward your mate.

Don't marry someone you can live with; marry someone you can't live without. That was the secret of the best friend. In the same way, if you have a best friend outside the marriage, know that you may well be entering treacherous waters. If you confide your deepest feelings about yourself and your spouse with someone outside your marriage, you have taken the right thing and put it in the wrong place. Intimacy belongs first and foremost in your marriage. This is the secret of insiders.

After Anita and I had been married about twenty years, both of our daughters left the nest for college. My wife and I took a walk one evening, and along the way, she shared something that surprised me. Anita speaks her mind and is what one of my friends calls "a pistol." She has a lot of fire. That's one of the traits that attracted me to her.

As we strolled through the neighborhood, Anita said, "I'm going to start speaking my mind now." I stumbled a bit and thought I had misheard her.

"What did you just say?" I asked with incredulity and confusion.

"I'm going to start speaking my mind now," she said again. "I've not always really shared my thoughts while the girls were home. We needed to have a united front with the kids. Now that the girls are gone, I'm not gonna hold back anymore."

I nearly fell over. For those twenty years, plus the years we had dated, I certainly never thought that Anita had held any thought back. Ever. Opinions flowed like water gushing from Old Faithful. She shocked me with the news that more were still to come.

But I'm glad she said it. I want her full self, and I want her honesty. She's my best friend. I do not want her to hold back. (As it turns out, in the years since she said that, I haven't really noticed any difference in her newfound "freedom of expression.") That is the nature of intimacy: the ability and freedom to share completely with your mate what you are thinking and feeling. And that sharing rightly belongs only within the marriage.

Having a "work wife" or a friend of the opposite sex with whom you share deep feelings quickly places you on the first stepping stone toward creating distance in your marriage. It may not seem like it at the time, but it often becomes the first movement toward an extramarital affair, either with that friend or with someone else. The power of intimacy, temptation, and seduction is real. Once intimacy begins to leave the building, it gets increasingly difficult for a marriage to recover its vitality.

Our family has lived in several very small communities. One had a rural school in what was really more of a village than a town. The community had a post office, a store, two churches, a school, and a fire station. The big field trip for the kindergarten class each year was to walk next door to the fire station and see the trucks and equipment.

One year when that field trip arrived, the teacher, Mrs. Smithson, and her assistant led the kids on the walk to the fire station. They oohed and aahed at the huge trucks. Mrs. Smithson had them sit in an open area, and introduced "Captain Bob." He led the team there at the fire station, and he stepped up to share a little bit about their work and what the children were seeing. As he stepped up, one of the five-year-old students shouted out, "I know Captain Bob! He comes to visit my mom when my dad's not home."

Needless to say, that little boy's mom and dad probably had not set out to lose intimacy and be unfaithful to each other. But somewhere along the way, one of them made a decision to look outside for inside help. And the results were not only awkward and embarrassing; they were disastrous.

As a couple, you have your own language, your own ways of communicating and interacting with each other. You probably have nicknames for each other. You have stories that only you two know. You have little words or turns of phrase that bring a chuckle because they spark special memories. Your relationship has its own collection of inside jokes. These are all signs of intimacy. You have bonded together as one whole.

When there are struggles in your relationship, as there are in all relationships, a natural urge will occur to look for help outside rather than inside the marriage. Be very careful when beginning to look for help outside the marriage. Of course, a trained, licensed, faith-based counselor can be helpful to you individually or as a couple. A caring friend of the same sex can sometimes lend a sympathetic ear and offer a word of encouragement.

In fact, having a regular relationship with a licensed, faith-based counselor or with your pastor can help you and the relationship in much the same way a good mechanic helps your car. Isn't it interesting that everyone agrees on the importance of doing some premarital counseling and equipping but very few people advocate the same kind of assistance once you are actually married? It's as if we believe that fairy dust is sprinkled on a relationship at the wedding, and every complication and frustration just magically disappears from that point forward. You and I know that is not the case.

When you buy a new car, it smells fresh, an aroma so pleasant that you can even buy air freshener to mimic it. At regular intervals, your mechanic inspects your car and does routine maintenance to keep it running safely and well.

After you've been driving your new car for two or three years, you hear an irritating noise. You're not sure what it is, but you know the car needs some attention. So you spend some time with your mechanic. After another year or two, you notice some leaking oil, and again you make an appointment with the mechanic. He or she helps you ensure that the small things do not become big things that cause your car to break down or even be destroyed.

However, if you ignore the regular maintenance, shrug off the irritating noise, forget about the leaking oil, and just keep on driving the vehicle, you will be in trouble. You will eventually find yourself with a blown gasket, a broken seal, or even a blown engine. The repairs will be in the thousands of dollars and you may even have to purchase a new engine or a new car. Simple, routine maintenance at regular intervals could have prevented the damage.

In the same way, routine visits for you as a couple to a counselor can help prevent deeper, long-term damage that can lead to divorce. Regular opportunities to talk and listen, while receiving the wisdom of an objective guide, will yield great results in strengthening your relationship. Communication workshops can help you along the way as well. Preventive maintenance produces far better results than waiting until the whole relationship has broken down. Most couples wait until it is too late before going to see a counselor. Preventive maintenance along the way could have made all the difference in the world.

Danger often arises when one spouse seeks help from outside friends who know the deepest intimacies of the heart that are being kept from a spouse. This transferring of intimacy from inside the marriage to outside it will often damage the relationship rather than help it. More important, if those outsider friends are of the opposite sex, the damage can quickly become so severe that the marriage cannot survive. A man who learns that his wife is emotionally confiding in another man, even without any physical intimacy, will feel betrayed.

If you feel you need the perspective of someone from the opposite sex in order to understand your spouse better, consider meeting with your pastor, having a marital counselor of that gender, or discussing your concerns with friends who are a couple so that you get both perspectives. Tread carefully before becoming emotionally intimate with someone of the opposite sex who is not your spouse.

The secret of insiders is simple: Do not look outside for inside help. Discuss routine maintenance together as a couple so that you can make the decision to find a good resource together. In that case, the decision will serve to strengthen your intimacy because you are working together. But looking to other friends or coworkers outside the marriage will often do more harm than good.

REAL-LIFE HELP

Make a promise to each other: "We will succeed. Divorce will never be an option for us." Then agree to do one of these three things sometime in the next three months:

1) *Add a date night to your calendar at least once every two weeks. Save this time just for the two of you. You may take a long walk together, go out to eat, see a movie, or simply sit on a bench and look at the stars while you talk. The point is, this time is only for the two of you. Consistent undivided-attention time will help preserve your deep friendship.*

OR

2) *Attend a onetime seminar or workshop on communication. Schools, churches, and counseling centers in your area will usually offer a half day or full day that teaches and refreshes on good communication skills. Many of these are offered free of charge. All couples benefit from doing constructive things together, and any couple will grow by learning to communicate with one another more effectively.*

OR

3) *Schedule one visit to a licensed, faith-based marriage counselor. All relationships benefit from an occasional tune-up, just like a car needs its oil and spark plugs changed on a regular basis. It is quite healthy for couples preparing to get married to select a professional counselor and promise to see that person once or twice a year after their wedding just to check in and "keep the oil fresh" in their marriage.*

14

THE SECRET OF ATTENTION
AND AFFECTION

Attention and affection work for a marriage like oxygen and water work for the human body.

When my father died a few years ago, my uncle, Dad's one brother, shared with me his favorite memory of my dad. My mother and father met when they were older than most people who married in that era. They both thought that marriage had passed them by, that they were too old. They met at church in Nashville,

Tennessee, and quickly began dating. Soon after, my mother moved six hours away to begin graduate school in chemistry.

My uncle beamed after my dad's funeral as he shared with me how my father had driven six hours each way every weekend for a year to see my mother. He said, "When we saw your father giving your mother that kind of attention, we knew this relationship was going to be the one!" Six hours each way, every weekend, for a year. That's giving someone your full attention.

When it comes to the secrets of a satisfying marriage, scientific research tends to confirm what faith has already taught us, which makes sense. After all, God designed the universe, and science helps us discover the intricacies of it. But I still find it amusing how the insights of today's researchers nearly always coalesce with the timeless wisdom of Church teaching and sacred Scripture.

And nowhere do science and faith coalesce more than in the secret of attention and affection. These two ingredients in a relationship work like oxygen and water in a human body. With them, it thrives. Without them, it withers.

One marriage researcher, Dr. Willard Harley, goes so far as to propose a strict policy of undivided attention in every marriage. Dr. Harley focuses most of his work on preventing and recovering from infidelity. His key to preventing infidelity? Give your spouse your undivided attention a minimum of fifteen hours each week. Use the time to meet each other's emotional needs of affection, conversation, recreational companionship, and sexual fulfillment. Very simply, the secret of attention and affection will prevent you from neglecting each other.

However, when attention and affection are largely missing, a relationship becomes like a ship in shallow water drifting toward the rocks. Years ago, I went to the doctor for my examination before having surgery. My regular doctor was unable to see me that day, so I met a physician, Dr. Vinson, I had never met before. And our conversation surprised me.

Dr. Vinson told me that she and her husband had recently separated. The two of them had lived together nine years, then they had married and shared that marriage for six more years, having two children in the process. As she reflected with sadness on the demise of their marriage and relationship, she said something so poignant I wrote it down some twenty-plus years ago and still have it to consider: "Our relationship has been dying a slow, gasping death since the day we married. You don't need love. You need intimacy, trust, concern. A relationship can do without love; it's the others that cannot be replaced."

I would disagree with her that a relationship "can do without love." That's probably because she is confusing love with the quickened heartbeat and breathless moments that really are more for the sizzle period of the relationship.

What really strikes me about her words is the desperate pining for attention and affection. "You need intimacy, trust, concern." She's right about that. Every relationship, every marriage, every person needs those: intimacy, trust, concern. What she was really saying was, "I yearned to be heard, to be paid attention to, to be loved. I needed attention and affection." We all do. Without those qualities, a relationship will wither and die.

From a faith perspective, the secret of attention and affection makes perfect sense. Remember God's purpose for marriage in the first place: "The Lord God said, 'It is not good for the man to be alone. I will make a suitable partner for him.'" (Genesis 2:18)

The secret of attention and affection should remind you of the secret of the love bank and the love languages. If a man desires to give love in a way that genuinely touches the heart of his wife, he will know that his wife probably desires quality time. What is quality time? Attention and affection.

Women need to feel special. Again, remember the provocative words of my wife regarding sexual intimacy: Women need a reason; men need a place. Women need and desire sex and physical intimacy also. But they arrive at that intimacy in a way that's different from that of men. Women need to feel special.

The secret of attention and affection makes that real. In fact, making your wife feel special can often be more simple than most men think. Give her your undivided attention. Look her in the eyes. Listen carefully to her thoughts. And more often than not, she will feel valued and heard.

A Leger–Canadian Press survey asked men and women what they most want in a spouse. Both women and men shared three of the top four answers: first, a faithful partner; second, respect for the other person's independence; and fourth, physical attraction.

However, the third-ranking quality differed. Men desired a woman with intelligence. Women desired a man with the ability to listen. There it is again: undivided attention.

One of my female friends summarizes it this way: Women are not carburetors, so quit trying to fix them. The secret of attention and affection means that paying attention trumps trying to fix her, the issue, or the problem. Just listen.

For many men, this runs counterintuitive to our fix-it mentality. But it dovetails straight into the words of Saint Paul we learned earlier: "Put on then, as God's chosen ones, holy and beloved, heartfelt compassion, kindness, humility, gentleness, and patience." (Colossians 3:12) The secret of attention and affection can be captured in those last three words: *humility, gentleness, and patience*. A marriage that contains these three elements is likely to succeed. A marriage without them will struggle for oxygen.

Yet, in a technological, wired world, gentleness and patience can be hard to find. Being accessible twenty-four hours a day and attached to a smartphone can prove toxic for gentleness and patience. Working men and women often master the art of being physically present but not truly present. Their attention, their emotions, and their patience are elsewhere because of the distractions of the world.

The cure is to listen slowly. One father, who realized he had failed to pay attention to his children, found himself sitting with his little girl. He invited her to share everything about her day, and to take her time and speak slowly. He really wanted to hear. His daughter replied, "OK, Daddy, but you are going to have to listen slowly too."

The same concept applies to marriage. Simply talking and listening actually matters—a lot. Open up to your wife with your thoughts and experiences. Show attentive affection by holding her hand, offering a gentle hug, sharing a smile, or praying with her. Offer these things on their own, not with sexual intentions.

As you do this, soon you will discover the power of silence. The two of you will grow so comfortable with one another that silence will not always need to be filled. You will enjoy being together for its own sake. Attention and affection can be shared without feeling obligated or anxious to fill up the time with words. The goal is undivided attention that makes each of you know that you are valued and cherished.

Walking into the post office, I encountered a longtime friend, Kevin. I hadn't seen him in years, and he looked awful. He mentioned that I looked like I had gained some weight (which I had, about twenty pounds). And I asked him if he was doing well, mentioning that he looked really tired.

Kevin had been enormously successful by the world's standards. He had started multiple companies from scratch, grown them to large sizes, and earned millions of dollars in the process. But now he looked drawn and pale.

When I mentioned that he looked weary, he said, "I tried to drink my way out of the recession. And I lost." He chuckled and we both smiled.

His pain was real, however. Kevin shared how he had lost his business and his home. In an effort to ease the pain, he had relied on alcohol, to the extreme detriment of his health. He then told me how he had just received a liver transplant. In addition to losing wealth and property, Kevin had also lost his liver. He had quit drinking entirely for well over a year to prepare for the surgery.

I asked him how the recovery process was coming along.

"Good news is I have my priorities realigned where they should be now. But I still have a lot of work to do to rebuild relationships with my wife. I've gotten my kids back into my life but still need to work on Lucy."

Clearly, in the chaos of an economic downturn and enormous financial pressure and losses, not to mention the humiliation of seeing all that you have built crumbling before your eyes, it is easy to make very poor decisions. Kevin had sacrificed his health and his most important relationship because he didn't have the emotional capacity or the time and energy to give his wife the attention and affection necessary to maintain any marriage, let alone one going through an extended period of pressure and strain. Fortunately, he now realized that he needed to rebuild that attention and affection if he wanted the marriage to make it. His family's future depended on it.

The greatest gift any couple can give their children is the gift of a good marriage. A stable, thriving marriage creates a sense of identity for children. They know their place in the world, which gives them a sense of confidence and security. A child feels free to grow and explore when he or she knows that the home front is consistent and predictable—no worries at home about Dad and Mom screaming at each other or hurling objects or insults around the house; no fears that Mom or Dad may not come home or that the child is in danger at home. A stable, secure home life gives kids the greatest likelihood of success in life. And the secret of attention and affection creates that.

REAL-LIFE HELP

Sit together for fifteen minutes tonight. No cell phones. No laptops. No television in the background. No distractions. Share with each other the events of your day. Listen slowly to one another. Invest in a little attention and affection.

15

THE SECRET OF WOMEN

Be a woman; your husband needs that.

Anita surprised me. She does that a lot.

When I asked her the secret of a thriving marriage, she replied, "Be a man. Your wife needs that."

"What does that mean?" I asked her in response.

"No matter how much our culture tries to make women into men, and tells us women that we can do it all, there are still times when a woman needs a man to be a man. To carry the load. To be the heavy with the kids. To stand up."

"Hmm," was my reply. I had not expected her to say that.

She's right. What she really was describing was the secret of women and the secret of men (coming in the next chapter). It may seem shocking to some folks in our culture, but women and men are different. In all kinds of ways.

Men and women are not the same. High school biology makes that plain. Of course, men and women are *equal*; we're all made in the image of God. However, equal does not mean *same*. We were made *for* each other, not *like* each other. God made men and women to be much the same, yet significantly and wonderfully different.

God made Adam and Eve for each other. As male and female, they complement one another. She brings certain strengths to the table, as does he. His testosterone is not her estrogen. Femininity is God's idea and His creation. Her femininity is not man's masculinity. A father is not the same as a mother. Being different is good; it means we complement each other and round out each other's lives.

Remember that marriage is a mystery. And one portion of the mystery is discovering how the two of you fit together. How you uniquely complement each other as only the two of you can do. No other couple is quite like you, and figuring out your uniqueness is akin to working to solve a mystery. It takes some work, some experimentation, and maybe even a sense of humor!

John Paul II described it this way in his "Letter to Women":

The creation of woman is thus marked from the outset by the principle of help: a help which is not one-sided but mutual. Woman complements man, just as man complements woman: men and women are complementary. Womanhood expresses the "human" as much as manhood

does, but in a different and complementary way. . . . It
is only through the duality of the "masculine" and the
"feminine" that the "human" finds full realization.

In other words, the masculine and the feminine together form
the fullness of humanity. There is not one without the other.

Every culture and society develops its own definition of the
details of femininity, but the basic biology remains the same.
Girls learn early that boys are different. Genes and hormones
cause boys to be generally more muscular, aggressive, and loud.
Little girls tend to be kind, compassionate, sensitive, and tender.
Anyone who has ever supervised a kindergarten playground has
seen this reality.

As real as these gender differences are, however, it is clear that
the categories can overlap. Deborah, Abigail, Ruth, and Esther
all provide examples of women in sacred Scripture who knew
how and when to assert themselves. Jesus, Jeremiah, David, and
Paul all displayed sensitivity, compassion, and an attentiveness
to the needs of others.

Now consider the most famous words of sacred Scripture on
the subject of marriage:

Be subordinate to one another out of reverence for
Christ.

Wives should be subordinate to their husbands as to
the Lord.

For the husband is head of his wife just as Christ is
head of the church, he himself the savior of the body.

*As the church is subordinate to Christ, so wives should
be subordinate to their husbands in everything.*

*Husbands, love your wives, even as Christ loved the
church and handed himself over for her*

*To sanctify her, cleansing her by the bath of water with
the word,*

*That he might present to himself the church in
splendor, without spot or wrinkle or any such thing,
that she might be holy and without blemish.*

*So also husbands should love their wives as their own
bodies. He who loves his wife loves himself.*

*For no one hates his own flesh but rather nourishes
and cherishes it, even as Christ does the church,*

Because we are members of his body.
*"For this reason a man shall leave his father and
mother and be joined to his wife, and the two shall
become one flesh."*

*This is a great mystery, but I speak in reference to
Christ and the church.*

(EPHESIANS 5:21-32)

Notice how Saint Paul's instructions and teaching on
marriage here focus mainly on the obligations and duties of
men to emulate Jesus. Six of the verses inspire men to love their
wives as Jesus loves the Church. Only two of the verses focus
on women.

Some folks blanch at the apostle's description of complementarity. Why do we react so strongly to these verses? Men are to love women like Jesus loves the Church. As a woman, what would it be like to be loved by a man the way Christ loves His Church? Can you envision that? What would your life, your relationship, or your marriage look like if that were the case?

Likewise, women are to love men like the Church loves Jesus. Men and women should "be subordinate to one another out of reverence for Christ."

In particular, women are called twice to be subordinate as the Church subordinates herself to Christ. These roles are lived out in daily life by what I have labeled the three N's for women, and the three P's for men (again, to be covered in the next chapter's secret).

The secret of women consists of the three N's: nourish, nurture, and nest. These N's are a practical way of expressing the Church's teaching on the unique role of women: "The woman, 'flesh of his flesh,' his equal, his nearest in all things, is given to him by God as a 'helpmate'; she thus represents God from whom comes our help." (*Catechism* 1605)

In her role, the woman represents God.

Women *nourish*. When a child is sick, she almost universally calls for her mother. That has been true in every culture, in every age. There simply is nothing like the love of a mother. Even in the most challenging of situations, even when the mother has abandoned her children, still there is a basic love and loyalty to that mother just by virtue of her role, or office, as mother. Mom is still Mom.

Perhaps because of the natural gift of feeding a child from her breast, perhaps because of the unique attachment that comes from having nourished a baby in the womb for nine months before birth, a woman, more often than not, is far more likely to consider first the basic necessities of the child. No one cares like a mother cares.

Women nourish. And women *nurture*. It is easy to make this statement rigidly, again forgetting that sometimes men bring these qualities to the table. Nevertheless, it is the norm that a woman makes the world softer and warmer for the family and particularly for a child. For a child, the world can be very prickly when this warmth and tenderness do not exist. When there is little attachment to the mother, a child often struggles to find intimacy with others and a place of security and identity in the world.

Men usually struggle to nurture at the level that women do. A good example of this can be seen in the studies mentioned earlier showing that most of the time men leave when the wife becomes terminally ill. As a rule, men fail to nurture as well as women.

No one loves a child like a mother loves. No one dreams for a child like a mother dreams. And no one hurts for a child like a mother hurts. That is why the scene of the Blessed Mother, Mary, near the cross as Jesus dies is so deeply moving. We all know that no one hurts like a mother hurts, and surely Mary hurt the deepest of all at that moment.

Again, John Paul II phrases it elegantly when he says:

> In the light of Mary, the Church sees in the face of women the reflection of a beauty which mirrors the loftiest sentiments of which the human heart is capable: the self-offering totality of love; the strength that is

capable of bearing the greatest sorrows; limitless fidelity and tireless devotion to work; the ability to combine penetrating intuition with words of support and encouragement.

(REDEMPTORIS MATER 46)

Women nourish. Women nurture. And women *nest*. Someone has to build the nest for the family. In order to thrive, every family and home needs a semblance of order. That will require organizing, cleaning, meal preparation, managing basic affairs and errands, and the like. Can men perform some of these functions? Of course. Do they tend to make the home orderly and consistent? Not frequently.

The most successful people I know, men and women alike, all operate by the basic principle of KISS when it comes to home life: Keep It Simple, Stupid. A simple home life makes it possible to thrive in a dark and chaotic world. Without that simplicity at home, adults, and especially children, will flail around looking for consistency and order and never find their bearings.

I ran into my young friends Stan and Jessica about eighteen months after they were married. I asked them, "How's it going? How's this marriage thing working for you two?"

Jessica is a very talented and educated young woman. She has a promising professional career. Yet she replied, "It's been interesting to me. All my life, I've been taught to be a career woman. But after we got married, we just fell into these roles. I cook the meals, I do the laundry, I scrub the toilets. Stan takes care of the cars and everything outside the house. We just fell into doing that."

I asked her, "Anything else surprise you about marriage?"

"Yes," she said. "It's funny. Stan comes home. I'll be fixing dinner. I put it out there and say, 'How about this ham and macaroni and cheese, huh? This says I love you.' Stan won't even miss a beat. He'll say, 'How about that paycheck I brought home? That says I love you.'"

For Stan, being a provider and consistently earning money for the family represented love for his wife in the same way that a warm meal and hospitable setting represented love to Jessica. She did not view her work or her job in remotely the same way that Stan did. For her, love flows in a caring, nested environment. So she created that.

Men and women complement each other's strengths in a thriving marriage. They make each other better. After all, the purpose is to help one another produce the fruit of love, joy, peace, patience, kindness, generosity, faithfulness, gentleness, and self-control. We're trying to help each other get to heaven. That's the purpose. We were made for each other. And men bring as much to the relationship as women do, just in different ways.

In a society that often tries to make men and women the same, it is important to remember the secret of women. More often than not, the three *N*'s will make or break a family or a child. They are not optional parts of a relationship.

Nourishing, nurture, and nesting generally come from a woman. They can occasionally come from a man, but that's rare. The three N's are her secret. And they are valuable, eternally so. In fact, they represent God.

REAL-LIFE HELP

For women only: Write down the ways you see yourself in the three *N*'s. Do you particularly excel at one of them? Is there one that your husband does better than you, where his strengths complement yours? Share these thoughts with your mate, and give thanks for the unique ways that God has made you to complement one another. You were made for each other.

16

THE SECRET OF MEN

Be a man; your wife needs that.

Anita shared her idea of the secret of a thriving marriage: "Be a man. Your wife needs that."

Remember how she added her explanation of that. "No matter how much our culture tries to make women into men, and tells us that we can do it all, there are still times when a woman needs a man to be a man. To carry the load. To be the heavy with the kids. To stand up."

What she was really describing was the secret of men. Men are different. We are not women. That should be obvious, but somehow it is being called into question often in the world right now. Again, high school biology provides all the evidence needed. Compared to a woman, a man generally has a smaller stomach, larger lungs, 20 percent more red blood cells, 50 percent greater physical strength, a shorter life expectancy, and a lower heart rate. He's also more likely to be left-handed, dyslexic, or nearsighted. And all those differences exist because of one tiny chromosome.

God made Adam and Eve for each other. As male and female, they complement one another. He brings certain strengths to the relationship, as does she. His testosterone is not her estrogen. In all our efforts to make men and women the same, we have forgotten how men and women are designed to complement one another.

For most relationships, that means the secret of men can best be described as the three *P*'s: protect, provide, and push. While these three *P*'s do not apply to every single relationship or man, they are the norm. Complementing one another in a relationship means that his strengths fill in the gaps where she is weak, and her strengths do the same for him.

Generally, a man brings the three *P*'s to the relationship as his way of complementing her three *N*'s. Of course, there are occasions when the woman may provide one or more of these *P*'s, just as the man may provide one or more of the three *N*'s described earlier. Men and women are different. Nature makes that obvious.

Men *protect*. Of the famous verses about marriage in Ephesians 6 shared in the previous chapter, six are devoted to the expectations for men. Only two focus on the expectations for women. God clearly expects a lot from men when it comes to marriage and how they will care for their wives. Consider again these words from Ephesians 6: "Husbands, love your wives, even as Christ loved the church and handed himself over for her."

Most men see themselves as the protectors of women. There is a reason for the stereotype of the valiant man rescuing the damsel in distress. That image appeals to men's physical strengths and prowess. Men need and desire to protect. We are hardwired that way.

Harry embodied that dimension in his marriage to Regina. He saw himself as her protector, so much so that their story made news across America. Harry and Regina enjoyed a truly lifelong romantic relationship. And they worked at it. They went to Mass together, prayed together, played cards together, and shared nearly every aspect of life. Attention and affection saturated their relationship. They had little habits, like on Saturday nights when they watched *The Lawrence Welk Show*, they'd sit on the couch together and hold hands and their children would help Mom up so she could sway because she loved to dance. Harry used to say that Regina could make any man look like a good dancer because she was so good.

The Ohio couple welcomed six children into the world, followed by fourteen grandchildren. Harold saw himself as Regina's protector over the course of their sixty-five years of marriage. He worked as a teacher, principal, and coach in the local school system; Regina worked as a school secretary after being a stay-at-home mom. They lived in the same home for decades, until they needed greater care and moved to another Ohio town to be near their daughter, a nurse.

In the nursing home, the caregiver would tuck Regina in each night and then Harry would go in and bless her with holy water and give her a kiss. That was part of their ritual. Harry praying and protecting her as the day ended and the night began.

Their daughter, Karen, said, "When Mom became ill, we tried to make it clear to Dad that Mom wasn't going to make it, and he seemed really agitated for a day or so, at first. And then he became really calm, and I think he decided, 'No she's not going without me.' Mom had said that she didn't want to be here without Dad. They were just so devoted to one another." He was her protector. She knew she could always count on him. He made her feel safe. She struggled to imagine a life without him at her side.

Harry died on a Sunday at seven thirty a.m., at the age of ninety-one. Regina died later that evening, at six thirty, at the age of eighty-nine. They both passed away in the room they'd shared for the past two months in a nursing home. Harry and Regina would have celebrated their sixty-sixth wedding anniversary the following week. Instead, they fulfilled their wish of crossing the river and going home together. "I think we all agreed it was no coincidence," said their daughter.

Perhaps best of all, their family decided to celebrate Harry and Regina's sixty-five-year union with a joint funeral Mass. The granddaughters carried Regina's casket; the grandsons carried Harry's.

Men protect.

Men also *provide*. Again, note the words from Saint Paul: "So also husbands should love their wives as their own bodies. He who loves his wife loves himself. For no one hates his own flesh but rather nourishes and cherishes it, even as Christ does the Church . . ."

Each of us wants to take care of our bodies. We do that with how we exercise, how we eat, how we dress, how we bathe. In the same way that a man provides for his own body, he will also desire to provide for his wife. Again, Jesus provides the example with how He cherishes the Church.

This providing does not mean that men do not appreciate the fact that women can work and add value and create things too. It reflects the fact that we are hardwired to provide for our wives and families. One research team, led by Shaunti Feldhahn, asked men how often they think about the need to provide for family. Three out of four said they think about that need often or all the time. It is almost always in the backs of our male minds: "As a man, I need to provide."

That same research team asked men if they would still feel an obligation to provide, even if their wives made enough so that the men did not need to work. Virtually all the men said they would still feel the need to work and provide.

I saw that in my father in a remarkable way. Dad talked very little, but he gave me many gifts. Most of those gifts I did not discover until I became a man and a father myself. Dad left our home every morning at seven thirty to go to work. He returned every day and walked through the door of our home at five thirty p.m. It was like clockwork. Dad walked to and from work, and his schedule and routine reigned supreme. We could count on him.

I never worried that my father would not return home. He always did, and at the same time. I never fretted that he would come home drunk. He never did. I never felt anxious that he would come home in a rage and take out his frustration on my mother, my brother, or me. His predictability and steadiness freed me from worry about the basic needs in my life. He provided for us, day in and day out. And that consistency gave my home life a peaceful stability. It was only after I entered full-time ministry that I discovered how often families and children lack that basic stability and how chaotic life is without it.

My father also said very little about his work. An accountant by training, Dad was a man of few words. And I will always remember the first time my wife, children, and I saw him after he retired. He and my mother came for a visit to our home a month or two after he had retired.

Over the years, my father had spoken very little to Anita. He loved her, but he kept his words to himself. And he usually interacted minimally with my daughters. But then he retired. When my parents visited that time, the change in my father was immediately apparent. He got on the floor and played with the girls. He talked with them, laughed with them, and spoke to us all. He probably said more in that three-day visit to my family than he had said in the six or eight years prior.

It took me a few days to figure out the transformation. For all those years of working, that male need to provide weighed first and foremost on my father's mind. I remember him missing work only one time in all my life. He wore that responsibility like a heavy mantle that he carried with him always. Gotta work. Gotta drive. Gotta provide.

But once he retired, his providing was complete. The mantle was removed. My father then became Chatty Cathy. He no longer was preoccupied with the need to provide.

My father was no alpha male. Unlike me, he was not a type A personality. But nevertheless, as a man, husband, and father, Dad was hardwired, deep down, to provide. And he carried that responsibility quietly in his own way each and every day. He believed that was a key part of his role in his marriage and in his family. Provide.

When we men do provide, we see it as a primary way of showing our love. Even Joseph, the earthly father of Jesus and husband of Mary, was a carpenter. He provided for the Son of God.

Men protect. Men provide. And men *push*.

Men and women complement one another in a thriving marriage. The mother usually nourishes and nurtures the child. She makes sure that the nest is warm, comfortable, and secure. In contrast, the man pushes the child. He encourages the child to explore and take risks. Usually, it is the father who teaches the child to ride a bike, to drive a car, or to camp out in the woods. These are risky activities. Men push the boundaries a little at a time so that a child can grow and develop. Pushing a child allows for the discovery of his or her strengths and weaknesses.

Again, risks are involved. It is the father who usually encourages risk taking and exploring, while the mother typically worries about a child being too far from sight. A man is wired to know that you cannot play it safe all the time or you will be dependent and unable to fend for yourself.

And in the end, it is usually the man who pushes the child out of the nest altogether at the appropriate time. Women make it comfortable to be at home. Men push the child and the boundaries because life and the world are bigger than the home. A mother helps the child feel secure, while a father helps the child stretch and grow. Complementarity.

In America, where nearly half of children are born into homes where there is no father, single mothers do heroic work. However, they face very real challenges. It is virtually impossible for one parent to fulfill both roles as nurturer and pusher. As marriage falls into chaos in our culture, it is more important than ever to take stock of the genius of God's creation, and how men and women really do complement one another in ways that cannot be replicated in any other way. According to the U.S. Census Bureau, children in absentee-father homes are four times more likely to grow up in poverty. On a spiritual level, these same children also are more likely to abuse drugs, drop out of school, and be incarcerated. The secret of men matters more than we may want to admit.

Men and women complement each other's strengths in a thriving marriage. They make each other better. After all, we're trying to help each other get to heaven in the holiest form possible. That's the purpose. We were made for each other.

REAL-LIFE HELP

For men only: Write down the ways you see yourself in the three *P*'s. Do you particularly excel at one of them? Is there one that your wife does better than you, in which her strengths complement your weaknesses? Share these thoughts with your wife, and give thanks for the unique ways that God has made you to complement one another. You were made for each other.

V. GRACE
SECRETS

Let me not to the marriage of true minds
Admit impediments.
Love is not love
Which alters when it alteration finds,
Or bends with the remover to remove:
O no! it is an ever-fixed mark
That looks on tempests and is never shaken;

WILLIAM SHAKESPEARE

17

THE SECRET OF SACRIFICE

Sacrifice is usually difficult and irksome;
do it anyway.

When Anita and I celebrated our twenty-fifth wedding anniversary, I asked my radio listeners to share with me the one secret to a long-lasting marriage. The calls poured in. Some were witty, some were nostalgic, some were regretful, and some were profound.

However, the one I remember the most came out as one sentence. The caller said,: "It's better to be happy than right." That's the secret of sacrifice.

Now that you've discovered the first sixteen secrets of marriage, the secret of sacrifice will make sense more than ever. This secret combines the remarkable example of Carlton and Maggie (from chapter 1) with the most powerful words of sacred Scripture when it comes to marriage.

Think back to Carlton and his unyielding love for Maggie. In particular, remember:

- *Carlton's leaving home to go earn money so he could provide a life for them as a couple*
- *His learning to make home brew when Maggie was struggling to produce breast milk to feed little Tommy*
- *His attention and care for Maggie as she contracted breast cancer, endured bone fractures, and needed more and more care*
- *His doing the laundry, the cooking, and the cleaning when Maggie became unable to help*
- *His going to the Hope Community Home to feed Maggie three times a day, then sitting with her in the familiar rocker next to her bed to put her at ease*

Carlton embodied the secret of sacrifice. He lovingly gave up himself in order to serve and aid Maggie. In fact, he later said, "I vowed to be with her until death do us part, and I was. Being with her when she died was the hardest thing I ever did, but it was also the most precious." That's sacrifice—hard but precious.

Love is best expressed in sacrifice.

That's exactly what Saint Paul is getting at in his words about marriage in Ephesians:

*Be subordinate to one another out of reverence for
Christ.*

*Wives should be subordinate to their husbands
as to the Lord.*

*For the husband is head of his wife just as Christ is
head of the church, he himself the savior of the body.*

*As the church is subordinate to Christ, so wives should
be subordinate to their husbands in everything.*

*Husbands, love your wives, even as Christ loved the
church and handed himself over for her*

*To sanctify her, cleansing her by the bath of water with
the word,*

*That he might present to himself the church in
splendor, without spot or wrinkle or any such thing,
that she might be holy and without blemish.*

*So also husbands should love their wives as their own
bodies. He who loves his wife loves himself.
For no one hates his own flesh but rather nourishes
and cherishes it, even as Christ does the church,
Because we are members of his body.*

*"For this reason a man shall leave his father and
mother and be joined to his wife, and the two shall
become one flesh."*

*This is a great mystery, but I speak in reference to
Christ and the church.*

(EPHESIANS 5:21–32)

Again, marriage reflects the union of Jesus Christ and His Church. The sacrificing love of God is our example and inspiration. After all, God sacrificed His son out of love. For any married couple, the perfection of life is love.

The woman is meant to be the helpmate of her husband. The man is meant to be the comfort and strength for his wife. Both of these roles require sacrifice in order for the marriage to work. To freely give up power is actually to have more. Again, the goal is not some power game but rather a love that helps your mate get to heaven and become the-best-version-of-themselves on the way. Love requires sacrifice.

In fact, Saint John Paul II spoke of the necessity at all times of not viewing your spouse as a means to your own pleasure and happiness. Instead, you pursue his or her well-being. You actively choose to do and say what is in his or her best interests.

In many ways, Ephesians 6 describes a much simpler challenge for women than what is outlined here for men. Husbands are to love as Christ loved. Christ gave Himself for the Church. Jesus gave everything. He emptied Himself. He gave up His place in heaven in order to become a human being in the flesh. He endured suffering and humiliation in order to love us. He was willing to die. That willingness flowed from a love so deep and so rich that we can barely comprehend it. Love sacrifices.

Men are called to do the same for their wives. Just as Richard (from chapter 2) resigned his prestigious role as president of a college in order to serve his wife, Mary, as she descended into the confusion and anxiety of Alzheimer's, Carlton reordered his life out of love and gave himself up to serve Maggie as her body broke down.

The apostle Paul describes this kind of sacrificial love as a man caring for his wife the way he does for his own body. And he grounds that example in the cross of Christ, the Savior of the body.

Often this lesson is discovered most when your spouse is sick and in need of bucketsful of your time and patience. When the moment of decision comes and you respond as you should—even without fully understanding—understanding emerges. Love grows. And you discover that *sacrament* means "mystery" for a reason.

Beth Holtz had birthed four children, welcomed nine grandchildren, and been married to Lou Holtz for forty-eight years when she was diagnosed with stage four cancer. She faced thirteen hours of surgery, eighty-three radiation treatments, and enormous suffering. Her children and grandchildren organized themselves to care for her and to encourage her. There were visits, prayers, cards, gifts, drives to the doctor's office, meals. In short, they rallied around their mother, who had generously served them and other people for decades.

When the storm had passed and she had survived the cancer, a reporter asked Beth, "What's the most important thing you learned from cancer?"

She replied, "I learned how much my family loves me."

When her husband heard that, he realized, "It's not that we loved her more; it's just that we actually showed it." That's sacrificial love.

Saint Paul shares that all of this is a "great mystery." The mystical union of marriage, rooted in love, displays itself most obviously in the sacrifice that a man and a woman routinely make for each other and for the good of their union. The two somehow do indeed become one. Men learn to love like God loves. Women embody the Church in its love and devotion to Jesus. Love is measured in sacrifice. Power is freely relinquished and love emerges in its place, a profound mystery.

That's what marriage is: a profound and beautiful mystery. The Church teaches this in a lovely way, in her instructions to the couple:

> And because these words involve such solemn obligations, it is most fitting that you rest the security of your wedded life upon the great principle of self-sacrifice.

> And so you begin your married life by the voluntary and complete surrender of your individual lives in the interest of that deeper and wider life which you are to have in common.

> Henceforth you will belong entirely to each other; you will be one in mind, one in heart, and one in affections.

> And whatever sacrifices you may hereafter be required to make to preserve this mutual life, always make them generously.

> Sacrifice is usually difficult and irksome.

> Only love can make it easy, and perfect love can make it a joy.

> We are willing to give in proportion as we love.

And when love is perfect, the sacrifice is complete.

(ARCHBISHOP WILLIAM O. BRADY, "INSTRUCTION ON THE DAY OF MARRIAGE")

"When love is perfect, the sacrifice is complete." Very simply, my radio caller was correct. "It's better to be happy than right." In countless interviews I conducted for this book, I was amazed how often the response to my question "What's the greatest secret of marriage?" came back as the simple words, "Yes, dear." In the Kingdom of God, as in marriage, it is more important to be loving than to be right.

The secret of sacrifice may be the most powerful secret of all. After all, Jesus embodied it in the Incarnation and in the cross. He still does so every day in the Eucharist.

REAL-LIFE HELP

For men only: Say yes for one day. Whatever your wife asks of you, say yes. If you see something that will benefit her, do it without asking. Just for one day, embrace the secret of sacrifice. Tell no one else what you are doing. And observe how the Holy Spirit swells within you as you quietly sacrifice some of your own time, money, or desires in order to love your wife as Christ loves the Church.

18

THE SECRET OF CHILDREN

Love, in its very nature, gives and creates.

For all human history, marriage has been linked with the creation of new life in children. Saint Augustine said children were one of the three "goods" (or blessings) of marriage, right alongside the blessing of fidelity and the beauty of the unbreakable bond.

How could it be otherwise? How does God show His love? By creating the universe and by creating new life. The Holy Spirit is the Lord, the Giver of Life. The love of God creates new life. So too will love in a marriage produce new life. This is the secret of children.

"Love, in its very nature, gives and creates. Love builds up" (1 Corinthians 8:1). "It does not destroy or tear down. Love does not rejoice over wrongdoing but rejoices with the truth" (1 Corinthians 13:6). Creating new life is just a natural outflowing of love. Love gives, love creates, love welcomes, love nurtures, and love nourishes new life.

The Dead Sea dies because water flows into its basin but cannot flow out. In the opposite fashion, the Red Sea thrives because as water flows in, water flows out. So too with love. Love cannot be contained. It must be shared and distributed.

Think of rainwater filling a birdbath from above. When the birdbath fills to capacity, it overflows and spills water onto the ground. In contrast, a sprinkler receives its water from the pipes and then liberally distributes that water all around. Better still, the sprinkler can be strategically positioned to send water exactly where the owner desires. And it can be moved to other dry areas where it is needed.

God's love operates in a marriage just like rainwater. If you try to hold on to all the love that flows from above, you become like the birdbath. You cannot hold it all, so it just spills out haphazardly. In fact, your attempts to hoard love can turn toxic because the love of God is designed not to be contained but to be generously shared. A thriving marriage operates more like a sprinkler. You receive the love of God abundantly, and then you share it generously with one another and with the people around you who need it most. And in its own way, that love creates new life.

The point is simple: Because God has first loved you, He calls you to imitate that love and share it. We are conduits of

God's love to other people. Your marriage is designed by God to be like a sprinkler. Your love may be distributed into the lives of the people and community around you. Your love may also spring forth in the creation of a new life (or lives) in children.

That is how God is. He exists not in a state of solitude but as a community of persons (the Trinity). God is three in one.

"And He is Love. In His very nature, by definition, God is Love" (1 John 4:8).

In other words, in many ways, God is like a family. He is continuously loving within Himself, and He expresses this in creating new life in creatures like us. Notice how when God creates human beings in the book of Genesis, He says, "Let us make man in our own image . . . male and female He created them." God is three, and He is one, at the same time. Just like a family of persons.

Frank shared with me how his grandfather Anthony immigrated here from Italy almost a century ago. Anthony settled in New York City, married, and had five children before he contracted tuberculosis. He was quarantined, much like a leper. One night, he snuck out of confinement and ran home, knowing the police would be looking for him to return him to the quarantine. Sure enough, the police found him as they looked through the door of his home and saw Anthony passionately hugging his six-year-old daughter. That little girl would eventually become Frank's mother. After that night, she would never again see her father, the man who had helped give her life. But she always remembered that he cast everything else aside to come to her in love one last time before he died. He could not help but share his love.

We are created male and female in the image of God. Husband and wife are called to live in a family of persons that reflects the image of God Himself. In other words, the same loving relationship between the Father and the Son that is personified in the Spirit is mirrored in a loving family of husband, wife, and children.

All this demonstrates the secret of children. Kids are not accessories to be worn and shown off by parents like a new purse or a pair of alligator shoes. Nor are they like pets. They do not exist for their parents' pleasure, entertainment, or companionship.

Children exist in and for their own right. Each child is made in the image of God every bit as much as the parents are. They are a part of the family equally as the Spirit is a part of the Trinity. Children are a blessing and a gift, not a duty or a burden. After all, Jesus said, "Let the children come to me; do not prevent them, for the Kingdom of God belongs to such as these." (Mark 10:14)

Saints Joachim and Anne helped each other become saints as a married couple. How did they do that? By welcoming the gift of their child, Mary.

Church tradition teaches that Joachim and Anne became parents late in life. Their love had not produced children for most of their marriage, but when the gift of a child did arrive, they welcomed her. They nurtured and nourished Mary. They protected and provided for her. And Mary became the Mother of God. Their lone child became the vessel through which Jesus entered the world. Salvation came into the world through Mary because Joachim and Anne understood the secret of children.

All in all, we know very little about Saints Joachim and Anne. Nevertheless, they are honored by the Church for their crucial role in our salvation. These two saints nurtured Mary, taught her, and brought her up to be worthy of being the Mother of God. Their teaching led her to respond to God's invitation in her famous Yes expressed in the words of faith: "Let it be done to me as you will." Their example as loving, generous parents gave Mary the model to use as she brought up her own son, Jesus. Their faith and steadfastness laid a foundation for Mary that allowed her even to stand courageously by the cross as her son was crucified. Joachim and Anne are models for all parents.

Clearly, not all couples will be able to conceive children. Those who do will count themselves blessed by their Creator and will watch their love come alive anew in the children committed to their care. Should their hopes of children be without realization, they will cling to each other all the more and know that they will find their joy and their happiness in mutual love and in the guidance of God's hand into other aspects of new life. Either way, the marriage and any children belong to God above all.

Children are not a choice. They are a natural outflowing of love. By its very nature, love gives and creates. Each child reflects the image of God and assists the family in a unique way in becoming more like the family of God, the Trinity. Blessed are the husband and wife who are given children in the flesh so that they may lead them to be the children of God.

This is the secret of children.

REAL·LIFE HELP

If you have been unable to have children in your marriage, spend time today in prayer asking God to show you ways that your marital love can give and create new life in a way He desires. That love may be best expressed in serving and giving generously to support abused children, or by providing nurture and protection for the children of a struggling family member, or in any number of ways. Your love is designed to be shared in new life. God has a plan in mind for you.

If you do have children, use the Prayer Process shared in the secret of bedrock. Focus today on the Gratitude portion of prayer. As a couple, say a prayer of thanksgiving to God for the gift of your child(ren). Ask Him to help you protect, provide, nurture, and nourish just like Joachim and Anne did for Mary. Your children are made in the image of God (even on their worst days!). God intends for you to become more like His family, the Trinity.

If you do not have children, use the Prayer Process and focus your prayer time as a couple today on step 6, Pray for Others. Pray for the children in your life, those in your extended family, those in your neighborhood, and the forgotten children in your community and in the world. Open your heart to God's heart for children.

19

THE SECRET OF LIFE

_When two become one, that "one" has
its own life._

In a marriage, there's more going on than meets the eye. After
all, two persons are being merged into one, and that occurs
nowhere else in this world other than in a marriage. It is unique.
And that new "one" has its very own life. That new "one"
contains the secret of life.

The marriage itself has its own life. There is no other couple
exactly like this man and this woman. No other couple shares
the same history, the same interactions, the same hopes and

dreams, or the same chemistry. And that new one life of a married couple is unlike any other human relationship. It is characterized by its exclusiveness (fidelity) and its permanence (unbreakable bond). And, of course, it can also be characterized by the creation of children.

When children arrive, the family grows into a new dimension all its own. The secret of life moves from the couple itself to the now-expanding family. No family consists merely of the individual members. Just as the one couple has a life in its own right, so too does the family unit take on its own existence as a whole.

Again, this is based on God, who has life within Himself as the Trinity. He is Three and He is One. In the same way, a couple is two and a couple is one. And while a family has multiple members, it is also one. And the life of the whole becomes the priority. This is the secret of life demonstrated in so many of the lives of the saints.

Saint Elizabeth of Portugal positioned herself on a mule between the opposing armies of her husband and her son, as a living invitation to peace. Saint Matilda humbly removed herself from her home in an effort to eradicate her sons' anger toward one another. Saint Monica unceasingly prayed her son, Saint Augustine, into the Church.

Saint Gianna lived that secret of life to its fullest. Gianna earned her medical degree and then searched for God's will to decide whether He was calling her to join her two brothers in the mission field in Brazil or to marry Pietro Molla. Eventually, during a pilgrimage to Lourdes on the feast of the Immaculate

Conception, it became clear to Gianna that her call was to marriage and the family.

Pietro was an engineer and Gianna's colleague in the charitable group Catholic Action. He and Gianna became engaged on Easter Sunday and married later that year.

After suffering two miscarriages, and being blessed with three children, Saint Gianna became pregnant again. Early in this sixth pregnancy, doctors discovered a dangerous cyst on her uterus. Gianna chose the treatment least dangerous to her unborn child and endured a risky and painful surgery to remove the cyst. The baby survived unharmed, and the pregnancy continued. When it came time to deliver the child, Gianna instructed the doctor, "If you have to decide between me and the child, do not hesitate: Choose the child." And little Gianna Emanuela was born on April 21, 1962. Tragically, a week later, Gianna died at home. Those around her said she died while repeatedly praying, "Jesus, I love you. Jesus, I love you." Paradoxically, in her dying, she personified the secret of life best of all.

Saint Gianna Beretta Molla was an educated woman, a doctor of the finest reputation. She also loved her husband and family to the fullest. Love is greater than knowledge. "Knowledge puffs up, but love builds up." (1 Corinthians 8:1) In the ultimate act of love on behalf of her family, Gianna followed the example of Jesus Christ, who "having loved his own . . . loved them to the end." (John 13:1) This holy mother of a family embraced the secret of life. She deeply understood that the whole is greater than any of the parts. And she also understood the love of God: that love gives, creates, sacrifices, and even dies.

Faithful to the commitment and sacrament she made at her marriage to Pietro, and heroically loving the "one" of her family, Gianna will forever be known for the words shared by John Paul II at her canonization Mass: "The extreme sacrifice she sealed with her life testifies that only those who have the courage to give of themselves totally to God and to others are able to fulfill themselves."

The secret of life is that a person is never so great as when he or she gives self over to the whole. That secret of life flows straight out of the secret of purpose, the very first secret of this book. Man and wife love and help each other get to heaven. They encourage and spur each other onward to become the-best-version-of-themselves. Saint Gianna inspired her family, and they in turn moved her to lay down her life out of love. The continuous flowing of love spurred each member on to become that best version, that holy self.

As a result, Saint Gianna's daughter, Gianna Emanuela, wrote, "All my mother's life has been a hymn to life, to joy, to God's love, to Our Lady, to her family, to her very near, to her beloved husband, my daddy, her beloved children and her dear patients."

Life lived as a hymn to God's love—that is the secret of life.

REAL·LIFE HELP

As a couple, discuss today how being a part of your family (whether as a couple or as a couple with children) makes you a-better-version-of-yourself. How does being a part of the whole help you be more holy as a person? Are there ways you sacrifice for the good of the greater "one"? Can you see times when doing so has not only helped the one but has also purified you?

20

THE SECRET OF FORGIVENESS

The most important word in a marriage,
and it's not love.

What's the most important word in a marriage? Think about it: the single-most crucial word for your marriage. What would that be?

Perhaps it is *love*. Or you might think the crucial word is *faithfulness*. Then again, *trust* is an important word. And so is *honesty*. *Commitment* is too.

But the most important word in a marriage is *forgiveness*. And along with forgiveness comes its spouse, grace.

Show me a marriage teeming with forgiveness and grace and I will show you a healthy, thriving marriage.

Why is forgiveness so important? Because your purpose is to help each other get to heaven. You are helping your mate grow in love, joy, and peace. You want your spouse to abound in patience, kindness, and generosity. You hope your beloved will delight in faithfulness, gentleness, and self-control. But along the way, you know he or she will stumble. Your husband is going to make mistakes. Your wife is going to slip up. And you know that you will too.

Forgiveness will wipe the slate clean. Grace will confront the failures, meet them head-on, and push the Reset button. Forgiveness and grace will offer a second chance and the opportunity to grow from mistakes rather than being crushed by them. The key of forgiveness opens the door to redemption.

When early Christians were baptized, they took off their clothes and entered the baptismal waters naked. After receiving that sacrament in the name of the Father, of the Son, and of the Holy Spirit, they walked out of the waters on the other side. The new believers then received a white robe, symbolizing the heavenly garments described in the book of Revelation. This baptismal transition represented the taking off of the old self, the old way of being and doing things, and putting on a new self, a new way of being in Christ Jesus.

When our mates fail to be the-best-version-of-themselves, we can seek revenge or justice. We can strike back out of our anger or disappointment. Or we can seek the way God has embodied for us in Christ Jesus, the way of absorbing the hurt and then releasing it. This way offers a second chance, a fresh start, redemption.

If you are going to spend the rest of your life with someone, the time to understand that he or she is going to disappoint you is now. Your spouse is not perfect, in the same way that you are not perfect. Original sin captures us all. How do you want your spouse to treat you after you have spoken an unkind word or failed to follow through on a promise? Would you rather receive angry rebukes or a word of grace that says, "I believe in you. I know you can do better. You are forgiven. Let's try again"?

No one has captured my heart with this understanding of marriage more than Millie, a woman I met on the phone when she called my radio show.

Millie made an awful mistake, and she wanted to come home. She desired no more, and she could accept no less.

Married at age eighteen, Millie grew restless ten years later. With three kids to care for, and all the weight of adulthood bearing down on her shoulders, she soon found excitement in the arms of another man. For four months, she met this man clandestinely, and their passionate love affair gripped her entire life, both body and spirit.

After four months of meeting her lover in motels and parked cars, Millie left her husband and three children. She moved in with her paramour. They set up house in the same town, just a few miles away from her husband and kids. Millie's husband was devastated, but he refused to give up on her, their vows, and their family. He wrote her notes. He left her messages. On one occasion, he physically picked her up and took her to church to meet with their pastor. But Millie rejected all of his efforts, even going as far as telling the pastor, "I don't need you. I don't want this. I am finished with all of you."

For nearly a year, Millie reveled in her newfound freedom. No kids. No responsibilities. Just the passion and thrill of being in love with someone new. Or so she thought.

On a Wednesday morning, Millie woke up, in more ways than one. That morning, reality sank in. Her mind focused, and she thought, "What have I done?" She knew. She was making the biggest mistake of her life. All the decisions of the past year collapsed around her. She had taken a man who loved her unconditionally, and the children they had created together, and ditched that on the side of the road like a used cigarette butt. The crushing wave of what she had chosen washed over her. And she decided, "I am going home."

Millie had no expectation that her husband would forgive her. She hoped he would at least welcome her. She merely wanted to come home, to be back in the orbit where she belonged. Whether she could set things right or not did not matter, because at least she would be home.

Millie pulled into the driveway and went to the front door. She heard the kids playing in the backyard and stood there on the doorstep for a very long time. It was Wednesday night, right before her husband and children would leave to attend church. After what felt like a decade, Millie knocked on the door. Her husband opened the front door and she could not look up at him. She was shaking and ashamed.

Her husband took the first step. He placed his hands on Millie's face and held her chin up. Looking into her face, he said, "Welcome home."

She responded, "I wanna come home."

And he pulled her small body to him, and that was it.

They prayed. Millie cried. He cried. They went to church that night. And their pastor, whom Millie had verbally dismissed and rejected those months before, threw open his arms and said, "Welcome home, Millie. I'm so glad you're here."

Those were only the first welcomes Millie received. Open arms soon came from her parents-in-law, as well as from other members of the church.

A week later, Millie discovered that she was pregnant. The news meant one obvious thing: She was carrying the child of her lover. Needless to say, she was broken by it. The gravity of her mistake crushed her world. One week home, one week of moving toward making things right, and now this, an unexpected and fully unwanted pregnancy with a child who could be a permanent reminder of the biggest mistake Millie had ever made and the very real and deep pain she had inflicted on her family. She knew what she wanted to do: end the pregnancy.

That evening, Millie broke the news to her husband.

Like he had done on the doorstep of their home a week before, he looked her in the eye and said, "This is going to be all right." Millie shared that she did not believe she could go through with the pregnancy. The pain of the living reminder of her adultery was simply too great to bear. He told her that they would make something wonderful from the pain and raise the baby together.

Fortunately, the paramour did not want anything to do with the child, and Millie and her husband now have a lovely four-year-old daughter. Her in-laws and closest friends, the handful

204 • *Allen Hunt*

of people who knew the complete story, welcomed the baby just as they had welcomed Millie home upon her return.

Some people know and ask Millie's husband, "How could you have taken her back? How could you have forgiven her?" He replies the same way each time: "You know, with all that Christ did to forgive me, how could I look at my wife, the woman He gave me to love, and say, 'You know, you've done something so horrible that I can't forgive you after all that's been forgiven me?'"

Her husband's generous forgiveness brought her home again, this time to stay. It brought a baby from potential death to life, a full-time mother back to her children, his soul mate back to him, and a future to everyone involved. Through forgiveness, Millie's husband created a future of memories that will include grandchildren not yet born and mountaintops not yet reached.

For Millie, the harder part has been to forgive herself. That has taken a few years.

In her words, as she shared with me on my radio show, "It's something that I still struggle with. A few months into the relationship with the other man I felt I couldn't go back home. I felt like I had gone so far beyond, I'd done too much, and I couldn't go back. I was too bad. I didn't deserve my husband, and the whole time he had made it known that he was waiting for me. He had left me messages. He had left me notes, saying, 'I'm not giving up on us. This is not where you belong and this is not who you are.' It was just so overwhelming."

For Millie, it became a perfect picture of who God is.

When did she feel forgiven by her husband? "The moment I showed up on the doorstep and said, 'I want to come home.' It was instantaneous. I knew it. I could see it in his face. I could see it in his eyes."

Millie assumed it would take a long time to build up trust and to do all of the repair work on her relationship. "I felt like it was going to be a long road, and it really wasn't. From the beginning, I would call him if I thought I was going to be late at work, and I would let him know where I was. But I never felt doubted, and he never threw it up in my face. There was never any of that. The hard part was forgiving myself."

When did she feel forgiven by God? "I knew. I knew when I asked. I think because of him. I knew when I went home. I saw that grace. I saw that mercy. It only comes from God. As humans, we do not come by that naturally. I don't think I could do that either. It's horrible to say now, but if the situation were reversed, I do not think I could do that. I don't think I have that in me. It was so devastating, and it was the most horrible, horrible thing. But my husband is now the baby's father. Yes. He is."

Millie found herself locked out of her own life, imprisoned by the tragedy of her decisions. Only forgiveness could provide the key out of that dark prison of pain. Everybody needs to forgive somebody. While a husband needed to forgive his wife, Millie also needed to forgive herself. Her husband's forgiveness, inspired by the forgiveness of God, opened the door and a path to a restored relationship and a unified future together as a family. His forgiveness did not make him forget Millie's mistake; it allowed him to move past it.

Forgiveness, however, needs to occur in the little things each day every bit as much as in the big things like Millie experienced.

When I lead Dynamic Catholic's Passion and Purpose for Marriage events, I invite the couples to do the simple exercise that is the Real-Life Help at the end of this chapter.

It goes something like this: The man and woman sit, hold hands, and face each other. The woman usually goes first and I invite her to say, "Please forgive me for _____." She should fill in the blank with a small, simple something for which she desires her husband's forgiveness. I instruct him to respond with only three words, nothing more: "I forgive you."

Then the spouses switch roles, and the husband asks for forgiveness.

Two days after leading one of these events, I received a phone call from an attendee, Mitch, who eagerly wanted to share with me what had happened during that exercise.

"I couldn't believe it. I thought I knew what my wife was going to do," he began. "Say something kind of generic. I'd give a basic forgiveness like you said and then we'd switch. But instead, she sat there for a long time in silence. I started getting nervous. Finally, she said, 'Please forgive me for being bitter.'"

Mitch went on. "I was taken aback. I had no idea what she was talking about. I didn't know what to say or do, so I said, 'What do you mean?'

"My wife continued, 'Two years ago, when we had that fight. Do you remember?'"

Mitch shook his head tentatively, not really recalling what she was describing.

"Well, that night you got up and stormed out of the bedroom. You went downstairs and slept in the guest room in the basement."

A light went on in Mitch's head. He remembered the argument. When he had gotten up out of bed, he had screamed at her, "That's it! I've had enough. I just can't take this life anymore."

She said, "Ever since then, I've wondered if you were going to leave us. I've been anxious. And I've become bitter. Please forgive me."

What had been just a onetime moment of frustration for Mitch had been a life-altering conversation for his wife. He realized that he and his wife really needed to learn how to communicate and resolve conflict better. He had not given that fight a second thought, while she had been continually reliving it for two years. And forgiveness was the place to start.

These seemingly little moments for Mitch were not so little for his wife. In fact, most couples face similar challenges. And the answer is forgiveness and grace sprinkled into a relationship on a day-to-day basis so that misunderstandings and disappointments do not fester and grow over time into bitterness and resentment.

Of course, you reduce the number of occasions for forgiveness by developing healthy conflict resolution skills. Mitch had just learned that these skills lie at the heart of any healthy relationship, especially marriage. Emotions impact your marriage for better or for worse. For example, some emotions, like anger and anxiety, have the potential either to enrich or to impede relationships. On the other hand, emotions like confidence, optimism, and enthusiasm normally make relationships healthier.

As a result, marriages that successfully manage anger and anxiety while also creating confidence, optimism, and enthusiasm will be more satisfying than those in which anger and anxiety get out of hand and prevent positive interactions.

It is important to realize that, in a way, emotions are like a virus that can spread from one person to another. In other words, you can "catch" your spouse's anger, fear, and anxiety. Similarly, you can also infect your partner with your confidence and enthusiasm.

The first step is to learn how to reduce and release. The Prayer Process provides a simple, helpful way to do this. Connecting with God at moments of high stress introduces divine power into a human situation. Prayer reduces stress and tension and also invites the Holy Spirit to increase self-control. Remember the nine fruit of the Holy Spirit from chapter 1: love, joy, peace, patience, kindness, generosity, faithfulness, gentleness, and *self-control*. That self-control gives you the ability to regulate your emotions. It also prevents you from catching your spouse's emotions on a bad day.

At the same time, this self-control allows you to keep proper emotional perspective, something that is typically lost when both partners are experiencing anger, anxiety, frustration, and fear. These emotions often lead to damaging behaviors, like a shouting match or storming out of the house. Further, when both partners experience them at the same time, the tendency is for the negative energies to feed each other, causing an accelerating spiral that fuels even more emotional turbulence.

When both partners can regulate their emotional levels, each is able to make calm interpretations of the situation. They then can free themselves from being negatively influenced by the other's emotions. As a result, you won't find yourself yelling back at your partner just because she yelled at you. Or you won't become anxious when your husband's anxiety about household expenses gets out of hand.

Staying relaxed in the face of these emotions allows at least one person in the marriage to keep proper emotional perspective and thus guide the marriage to healthier and happier grounds.

Healthy conflict resolution is important in all relationships. But not all issues can be resolved purely through conflict skills. That is when forgiveness enters the scene and offers the opportunity for a reset.

Just like God does for us, a spouse can offer forgiveness, redemption, and the chance to move forward into a better future. Forgiveness comes from grace. It produces more love and more peace. No marriage will survive long without it. With it, a marriage will prosper.

That's why *forgiveness* is the most important word in a marriage. That's the secret of forgiveness.

REAL·LIFE HELP

As a couple, sit facing each other. Join hands. Look one another in the eye. Take turns doing the following exercise.

Let the wife go first.

As you look at your husband, say, "Please forgive me for _____," and then complete the sentence. Do not add an "if" or a "but." No explanations—just a simple apology for something done or said that you regret. It is best if this is something from the past week rather than dredging up issues from the distant past. Start anew with a fresh breeze of grace.

Husband, looking at your wife, simply say, "I forgive you." Add nothing else. Just receive her apology and offer forgiveness. Begin again.

Now reverse the roles, with the husband apologizing and the wife forgiving.

This simple act will help push the Reset button and begin a new habit of simple grace and forgiveness. This habit can be a game changer for your marriage.

Resist the temptation to expand the conversation in this exercise. There will be plenty of time later to have longer discussions. The goal right here and now is simply to learn to apologize and to forgive well. No more, no less.

21
THE SECRET OF 8

When you struggle, focus on the 8.

The final secret comes from a Roman prison. That may seem like an odd place to learn about marriage, but you'll quickly discover why it is actually the perfect location for this secret.

A deeply satisfying marriage takes work. Often, it requires a lot of work. That is just how love is. Love is a decision and an action, not merely a feeling or a quickened pulse.

So, what's the final secret that will help pull all these secrets and Real-Life Helps together in order to make a thriving marriage most likely to happen? That is the secret of 8.

Learn the secret of 8 and it will open an entirely new dimension in your marriage. This secret holds the potential to change the bad habits in your relationship into healthy ones.

Now, on to the Roman prison. I have visited more than one friend or family member in prison. I have no great desire to spend any extended time there even though television, electricity, water, three square meals per day, and heat are all provided. Roman prisons in the first century had none of those things. Usually they were underground, like caves. No natural sunlight could get in. The space was so dark that often prisoners would go stir-crazy and lose their minds.

In a Roman prison, men and women were kept together—in the dark, with no heat other than an occasional fire for light, but then the prisoners had a huge problem of smoke in an underground space with no ventilation. Ancient reporters told of hearing wailing and moaning emanating from the underground prisons as they walked by.

There were no long-term sentences. The Roman prison was more like a holding tank where you waited until your trial arrived, if it ever did. More often than not, prisoners starved to death unless they had someone on the outside to visit and bring food. Early Christians used the same words to describe hell as ancient writers used to describe prison: dark, dank, dismal, wailing, moaning, and filled with death.

All this darkness makes the words of Saint Paul all the more remarkable. To the Philippians, he wrote a letter from prison. Surrounded by darkness, hopelessness, death, wailing, moaning, and starvation, Saint Paul uses the word joy twelve times in a short letter that contains only four chapters. In the most joyless place on earth, the apostle describes joy twelve times! Here are just a few examples:

> *1:4 In all my prayers for all of you, I always pray with JOY*

> *2:18 So you too should be glad and REJOICE with me*

> *3:1 Finally, my brothers, REJOICE in the Lord*

> *4:4 REJOICE in the Lord always. I will say it again: REJOICE!*

Evidently, Paul thought Christians should be known for their joy. How in the world do you do that? How do you radiate joy, even in a Roman prison?

For you and me, the question is how to have a marriage permeated with joy, even on our worst days. The apostle Paul describes how to get to that kind of life: "Finally, brothers, whatever is *true*, whatever is *honorable*, whatever is *just*, whatever is *pure*, whatever is *lovely*, whatever is *gracious*, if there is any *excellence* and if there is anything worthy of *praise*, think about these things." (Philippians 4:8)

What's the answer? Redirect your mind. Our thoughts determine our lives. When our thoughts change, our lives change. When our thoughts change, our relationships also change.

Redirect your thoughts and your actions to the 8: true, honorable, just, pure, lovely, gracious, excellent, and praiseworthy. At our house, we call these THJPLGEP, by remembering the first letter of each of the 8 words. But THJPLGEP is really hard to say and to remember! So I've found it's easier to call it the secret of 8. These 8: True, honorable, just, pure, lovely, gracious, excellent, and praiseworthy.

We've already discovered that a healthy marriage bears the fragrance of grace, forgiveness, and love. And the secret of 8 allows you to sprinkle those virtues throughout your marriage, even in challenging moments.

When you are frustrated, when things in the marriage are less than ideal, when your spouse is stepping on your very last nerve, ask the Holy Spirit to redirect your mind. Think about the parts of your spouse, your marriage, and your relationship that are true, honorable, just, pure, lovely, gracious, excellent, and worthy of praise. Instead of the frustrating, the disappointing, the mundane, or the infuriating, redirect your thinking and your heart to the excellent.

Think about the 8: true, honorable, just, pure, lovely, gracious, excellent, and praiseworthy.

In other words, give your mate the benefit of the doubt. Rather than assuming the worst or operating with a suspicious or heavy spirit, remember what brought you together in the first place, remember your vows, and remember what is honorable about your spouse. Remind yourself that he really does love you, even if you are bothered by something at the present moment. Redirect your mind and heart to the fact that she has so much loveliness and graciousness even if she has pushed your buttons in the here and now.

Jack has been a divorce attorney for decades. He married once, and the marriage blew up within the first year. His negative experience in that divorce caused him to redirect his law practice to focus exclusively on representing men in similar situations. He spends most of his professional life dealing with highly contentious, inflamed relationships as the parties struggle to inflict one last deep wound before closing the door on their marriage. As a result, Jack offers a uniquely jaded view. He often tells me, "Never marry. Allen, you deal with people as they *should* be; I deal with people as they *really* are. I tell you, never marry."

Jack's is a cynical, legal view of marriage. But he's at least partially right. As Catholics, we surely deal with people as they *should* be—and not just that they *should* be, but that they *can* be. That's really the whole point, isn't it? We know that we are sinful creatures, but we do not have to remain that way. Our souls may have blemishes, and our relationships may have flaws, but those blemishes and flaws need not have the last word. The love of God, the Holy Spirit, and the sacraments give us the tools to become better-versions-of-ourselves. Remember the secret of purpose. We know where we are going (heaven), and we have the capacity to change and to grow. That's what our faith equips us to do.

Change and grow—that is exactly what the secret of 8 allows you to do. When you find yourself trapped in negative thinking about your spouse, something he has said, or something she has done, let that moment be a trigger. That trigger kicks in and causes you to redirect to the 8. Shift your thinking to the true, honorable, just, pure, lovely, gracious, excellent, and praiseworthy in your spouse and in your relationship. Change out of a bad habit and way of thinking and grow into a new one based on the 8.

A big fight or a few weeks of poor communication in a marriage can create a crisis. The little positive interactions are missing. Attention and affection are nowhere to be found. Somewhere in that crisis, you and/or your spouse realize something has to be done. Something has to change. The marriage needs to find its way back into health and wholeness again.

Crisis can begin that change, but triggers continue it. By using each negative thought as a trigger to redirect your mind and thoughts to the 8, you will build a new routine. And that routine gradually develops you into a-better-version-of-yourself and your marriage into the-best-version-of-itself.

When you stop, remember, and redirect to the 8, your marriage will slowly begin to fill up with grace. Grace, forgiveness, and love will soon follow.

When you are focused on the 8, you set the expectations high rather than low. You aim at the best rather than the worst. You expect the true, honorable, just, pure, lovely, gracious, excellent, and praiseworthy. And most of the time, people live and love up or down to the expectations we have for them. The 8 will focus you on the positive, cause you to expect the positive, and lead to the positive.

That is the secret of 8.

REAL-LIFE HELP

This final Real-Life Help will set the stage for the days and years to come. You now know the twenty-one undeniable secrets of marriage. You have begun to embrace them as a couple and to live them out in a new way through the Real-Life Helps.

Now comes the time to seal the deal.

As a couple, kneel together on the floor or a kneeling rail at your church. You might even kneel before a statue of the Blessed Mother or the Holy Family. Quietly say this prayer together aloud to the Lord. As you do so, peacefully invite the Holy Spirit to saturate your life as a couple as you make a new start together each day.

PRAYER OF HUMILITY

Lord
Help me to be humble
For I have wandered
Far from Your goodness and lived just for myself
Give me the courage to be self-effacing and honest

Forgive me for the times I have imprisoned myself
In selfishness
In greed
In envy
In arrogance
In anger
In despair

In mistrust

Forgive me for falling into
Self-pity
Self-doubt
Self-destruction
Self-containment

May these times of falling and failing
Lead me to a greater understanding of myself
And a new appreciation of Your infinite goodness and
mercy

Unbind me

From the dark clouds that veil my life in fear
From the allurement of empty promises
From self-satisfaction
From the paralysis of self-loathing

To be humble
Is to come close to You
Who desires nothing more only
To love us as You do

Heal the deepest places of hurt
So that nothing is hidden from You
And the gaze of Your gentle eyes

In my sorrow
May I listen to the words of those
Who seek forgiveness from me
May I accept the sincerity of their hearts
So they too will know Your healing mercy
Through my pardon

Lord
Forgive my blindness
In failing to see Your abundant blessings
Given daily from Your kindness

Forgive me Lord
That I would live again.

(FR. LIAM LAWTON)

WE CAN DO NO GREAT THINGS; ONLY SMALL THINGS WITH GREAT LOVE.

Blessed Teresa of Calcutta

THE SACRAMENT
OF MATRIMONY SIGNIFIES
THE UNION OF CHRIST
AND THE CHURCH. IT GIVES
SPOUSES THE GRACE TO
LOVE EACH OTHER WITH
THE LOVE WITH WHICH
CHRIST HAS LOVED HIS
CHURCH; THE GRACE OF THE
SACRAMENT THUS PERFECTS
THE HUMAN LOVE OF THE
SPOUSES, STRENGTHENS
THEIR INDISSOLUBLE UNITY,
AND SANCTIFIES THEM ON
THE WAY TO ETERNAL LIFE.

Catechism of the Catholic Church 1661

NOTES

NOTES

THE
DYNAMIC CATHOLIC
INSTITUTE

[MISSION]

To re-energize the Catholic Church
in America by developing world-class
resources that inspire people to
rediscover the genius of Catholicism.

[VISION]

To be the innovative leader in the
New Evangelization helping Catholics
and their parishes become
the-best-version-of-themselves.

DynamicCatholic.com
Be Bold. Be Catholic.®

The Dynamic Catholic Institute
5081 Olympic Blvd
Erlanger, Kentucky 41018
Phone: 859-980-7900
Email: info@DynamicCatholic.com